Contents

6 Introduction

10 CHAPTER I: THE OLD TESTAMENT

12 Eve
Forever remembered as the mother of the human race

18 Sarah
An unlikely child late in life produces joy and laughter

22 Hagar
Twice she is saved by the action of a compassionate God

24 Rebecca
Wily and resourceful, she takes matters into her own hands

30 Leah
A loveless marriage is salvaged by her bond with her children

34 Rachel
She gives birth to Joseph, the next great patriarch

38 Shiprah & Puah
The brave midwives help to thwart the Pharaoh's evil plan

40 Jochebed
The mother of Moses makes a sacrifice and trusts in God

42 Miriam
The sister of Moses is part of his story from the beginning

46 Zipporah
The foreign-born wife of Moses saves her husband's life

48 Mahlah, Noa, Hoglah, Milcah & Tirzah
The daughters of Zelophehad fight for their rights

50 Rahab
A Jericho harlot paves the way for an Israeli victory in Canaan

52 Deborah
Very few leaders filled as many roles as this dynamic figure

54 Jael
Her cold-blooded killing of an enemy helped God's people

56 Ruth & Naomi
Loyalty and compassion stand at the center of their tale

62 Delilah
Samson is undone by love and the wiles of a beautiful woman

64 Hannah
A desperate temple visit leads to the birth of a great prophet

66 Bathsheba
Lust led to transgression, but God's forgiveness saves the day

68 Tamar
A shocking rape ruins a life and leads to years of conflict

70 Jezebel
Her very name has come to represent treachery

72 Jehosheba
The princess's rescue of an heir preserves the house of David

74 Huldah
She exemplifies the importance of listening for God's voice

76 Abigail
Her negotiation skills help save her husband's life.

78 Esther
Her courageous action turns the tables on a dangerous enemy

80 The Nameless
Women who play significant roles in biblical narratives

88 CHAPTER II: THE NEW TESTAMENT

90 Mary
She remains an iconic figure for Christians all over the world

102 Mary Magdalene
Jesus's most loyal supporter follows him even to the tomb

110 Elizabeth
Mary's cousin is the first to recognize the divinity of Jesus

112 Martha
After chiding a tardy Jesus, she witnesses his greatest miracle

114 Salome
Her performance leads to the martyrdom of an early Christian prophet

118 Tabitha
The believer is brought back to life by Peter's prayers

120 Junia
A valuable leader stirs debate over her real gender identity

122 Lydia
The successful businesswoman helps to spread Jesus's teachings

124 Priscilla
Widely traveled, she played a major role in the early church

126 Phoebe
The pillar of early Christianity becomes Paul's emissary to Rome

128 The Saints
In the centuries since Jesus walked the earth, these female spiritual figures have continued to spread his message

138 CHAPTER III: MODERN SPIRITUALITY

140 The Shrines
A love for Mary is showcased in these sacred locales around the globe

150 Mother of Mercy
The Blessed Virgin is said to have appeared in many surprising places

160 A Tour of the Holy Land
Explore the places where key figures from the Old and New Testament lived and prayed

The Madonna and Child (The Mackintosh Madonna), by Raphael, 1510-1512

Mary (in blue) was comforted by a host of women after the Crucifixion of Jesus.

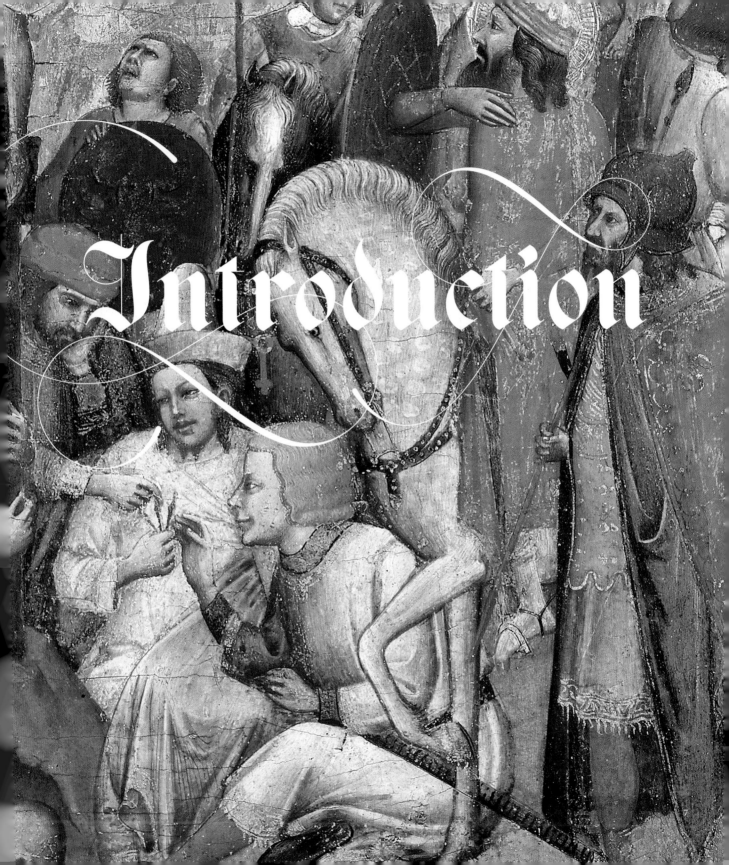

Introduction

The women of the Bible are a truly fascinating group. At one end of the spectrum, there are the women who will forever be paragons of virtue and faithfulness to the will of God. Mary, the mother of Jesus, of course, is first among this group. From the moment we meet her in the Gospels, she is depicted as soft-spoken, thoughtful, respectful and sweet. After the birth of Jesus, upon hearing the many prophecies and wonders to be associated with her son, she does not respond with shouts of joy or expressions of skepticism. No, quiet, tender Mary responds in her own distinctive way. "But Mary treasured all these words," the Bible tells us, "and pondered them in her heart." Ruth is another shining figure of pure goodness, whose devotion to her widowed mother-in-law, Naomi, has inspired biblical readers for centuries.

At the other end of the spectrum is a small coterie of villains, whose actions mark them for eternal condemnation. Delilah, the betrayer of Samson, who stole his strength and handed him over to the Philistines in exchange for money, is one of these. So is Jezebel, who killed God's priests and sought to convert the nation of Israel to the worship of Baal. Salome, whose seductive dance led to the execution of John the Baptist, must be put in this group, too—although her age and the strong influence of her mother should be considered mitigating factors.

The largest group—composed of fallible human beings struggling to respond to the will of God and their frequently challenging circumstances—lies between these two poles. Certainly all the great matriarchs in the Book of Genesis fall into this category. Sarah, unable to conceive, makes the Egyptian slave Hagar her surrogate, then mistreats Hagar when she does what is asked of her and bears Abraham a son. In the linked stories of these two women, we see God's agency in securing the futures of both: Sarah, though advanced in years, conceives and gives birth to Isaac; and an angel of the Lord saves Hagar's life in the wilderness and promises that her son, Ishmael, though wild and contentious, will become the founder of a great nation, too. Rebecca uses rank deception to secure a blessing from Isaac for her favored son, Jacob, but in so doing she ensures that God's plan for the future people of Israel remains on track. The sisters Leah and Rachel are two sides of the same coin—Leah struggles with a husband who does not love her, but six of the 12 future tribes of Israel descend from her; Rachel struggles with infertility but late in life God grants her wish to conceive and she gives birth to Joseph, who becomes the next in the long line of patriarchs who carry on the chosen people's sacred covenant with God. In all these instances, we see imperfect people who—sometimes by using their wits and sometimes with direct assistance from God—play important roles in advancing the divine plan.

Again and again, these narratives tell us, we are bound to fall short, but in the end a contrite heart and a faithful spirit will triumph through the grace of God. It is an ancient message, but one that resonates with believers to this day.

Here the Virgin is depicted as the Madonna of Misericordia, who offers protection to Christians who pray for her intercession.

9

Moses' sister Miriam led the women in a spontaneous celebration, complete with pipes, drums and tambourines, after their escape from Egypt.

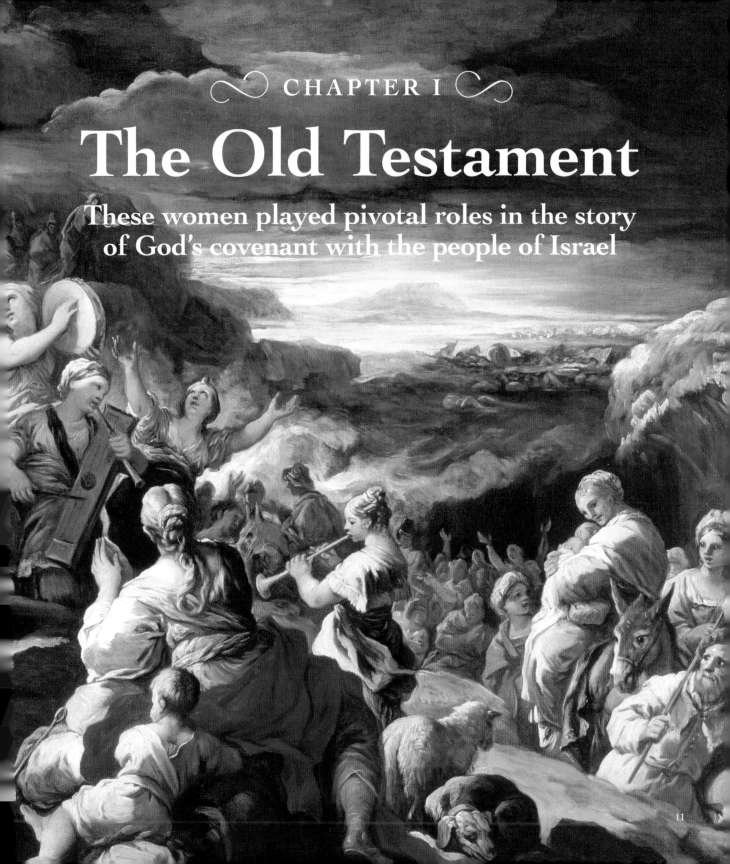

CHAPTER I

The Old Testament

These women played pivotal roles in the story
of God's covenant with the people of Israel

The "wily serpent," depicted here as a satanic figure, persuaded Eve to eat the forbidden fruit.

"So when the woman saw that the tree was good for food, and that it was a delight to the eyes, and that the tree was desired to make one wise, she took of its fruit and ate."

GENESIS 3:6

Eve

The First Woman

She will forever be remembered as the mother of the human race

Her name in Hebrew means "source of life." She was the first, the original woman, the mother of all humankind. As such, Eve will always be among the most prominent female figures in the Bible. The Book of Genesis includes two accounts of her creation—in the first, simpler version in Chapter 1, male and female are created simultaneously: "So God created humankind in his image, in the image of God he created them; male and female he created them." In the second, more familiar account in Chapter 2, man is formed from the dust of the Earth and woman is created from the rib of man. Some biblical scholars argue that even in this second account, the original man— *adam,* a non-gender-specific designation in Hebrew best translated as "humankind"—only becomes masculine after the rib has been removed and the

second human has taken shape, again suggesting a simultaneous formation of the two genders as we know them. In any case, there follows the famous tale of the wily serpent—"more crafty than any other wild animal that the Lord God had made"— who approaches Eve and talks her into eating the fruit of the tree in the middle of the Garden of Eden, where the first couple has been living in blissful union with God. God had told them that they would die if they were to eat the fruit or even touch the tree, but the serpent tells them, truthfully as it turns out, "You will not die; for God knows that when you eat of it your eyes will be opened, and you will be like God, knowing good and evil." Eve eats and quickly persuades Adam to partake as well. And indeed their eyes are opened—they suddenly become aware of their nakedness and

"So the Lord God banished him from the Garden of Eden."

GENESIS 3:23

quickly fashion clothing from fig leaves to cover themselves. God confronts the couple with their transgression and the buck-passing begins. First Adam blames Eve, and then Eve blames the serpent. God's condemnation is swift: The snake is condemned to slither on its belly (presumably before God's judgment, the snake had limbs), Eve is destined to suffer pain in childbirth and to be ruled over by her husband, and Adam is forced to toil endlessly to bring forth crops from unforgiving soil. Then the couple is driven from the garden, away from paradise and their lives of happy but ignorant innocence.

For some Christians, the story presents humanity's "original sin," the primal act of disobedience that could only be redeemed by the sacrifice of Jesus many years later. In this view, the serpent is often seen as Satan, and Eve as the first person to succumb to his temptations. Others see the tale as the biblical explanation for human consciousness, for our move from childlike innocence to full personhood, capable of moral reasoning and hence subject to God's judgment. In this interpretation, Eve is a vital figure in humanity's spiritual development.

The Bible is largely silent about the rest of Eve's life. We know she had two sons: Cain, a farmer, then Abel, a shepherd. And we know that Cain, jealous of his brother's standing with God, killed Abel and was condemned by God to "be a fugitive and a wanderer on the Earth." We can only imagine Eve's pain at these events, but with one son killed and the second a fugitive, she is blessed with a third named Seth, whose descendants would include Noah and the rest of humankind.

For their act of disobedience, Adam and Eve were condemned to "painful toil" for the rest of their lives.

17

Sarah was the first in a long line of strong and capable wives who supported—and sometimes deceived—the great patriarchs in the Book of Genesis

Sarah

A Promise Fulfilled

An unlikely child very late in life produces joy and laughter

The story of Sarah and her husband Abraham is a tale of two fallible and frequently faithless human beings stumbling their way through a series of challenges, seemingly on the edge of disaster, only to be redeemed by the action of God. The consistent message is that God will find a way to fulfill his covenant with the future people of Israel, no matter how flawed his human partners in the exercise may be. God's promise to Abraham is clear and unequivocal: "I will make of you a great nation, and I will bless you, and make your name great, so that you will be a blessing. I will bless those who bless you, and the one who curses you I will curse; and in you all the families of the Earth shall be blessed."

The first challenge the couple faces is a famine that forces them to move to Egypt to avoid starvation. Abraham, fearful that Sarah's beauty will persuade an Egyptian to murder him and steal his wife, decides to present her as his sister to save his own skin. She does indeed attract attention, from the Pharaoh of Egypt no less, and Abraham allows her, essentially, to be taken into his harem. The Bible does not tell us how Sarah felt about this arrangement, but both halves of the couple show a lack of faith in God's promises by going along with it. (As the patriarch in a patriarchal culture, Abraham clearly deserves the lion's share of the blame.)

God is displeased with this development and smites "Pharaoh and his house with great plagues

> *"The Lord dealt with Sarah as he had said, and the Lord did for Sarah as he had promised. Sarah conceived and bore Abraham a son in his old age....Abraham gave the name Isaac to the son whom Sarah bore him."*
>
> *GENESIS 21:1–3*

because of Sarah," causing Pharaoh to ship Sarah back to Abraham and send them both packing, along with the rather substantial amount of property Abraham has amassed during his time in Egypt. The human side of the covenant is found wanting, but the divine partner redeems the situation.

Many years later, Sarah still has not conceived. This time it is she who shows a lack of faith in God's promises as she decides—in keeping with the customs of the era—to send her servant (slave) Hagar to Abraham, in hopes that Hagar can bear the child that Sarah believes she cannot. This decision creates considerable pain for both women—and particularly for Hagar, who twice is nearly killed in the wilderness before God's intervention saves the day. Sarah, too, despite her unbelief, is redeemed by God, as she miraculously conceives at last—she laughs at the prospect when she hears God's promise, transmitted to Abraham by three divine messengers—and gives birth to Isaac, the next in Israel's line of patriarchs. "God has brought laughter for me," Sarah says, "everyone who hears will laugh with me. Who would ever have said to Abraham that Sarah would nurse children? Yet I have borne him a son in his old age."

This 1875 painting depicts Sarah and Abraham's reunion after the Pharaoh allowed her to return to her beloved husband.

21

Hagar
Suffering Servant

Twice she is saved by the action of a compassionate God

The story of Hagar, a poor Egyptian slave girl caught up in the machinations of Sarah, wife of Abraham and one of the great matriarchs of the Israelites, remains among the most poignant in the Bible. It is a tale of jealousy, cruelty and lack of faith, but in the end the compassion God shows Hagar salvages the tale from tragedy. As is often the case, the Bible recounts the tale simply, with a minimum of melodrama. Sarah has grown old and increasingly skeptical of God's promise to Abraham that his offspring would be as widespread as "the dust of the Earth" and would possess a great land. So she enlists her servant Hagar to be her surrogate and to give birth to the son who will fulfill God's promise. Abraham, according to custom, must accept this relatively common arrangement, though in doing so he, too, displays a lack of faith in God's promise.

After she becomes pregnant, according to some translations, Hagar "looked with contempt upon her mistress," though many scholars contend that the Hebrew verb simply suggests that Hagar no longer looked up to her mistress as she once did. In any case, Sarah is angry that her lowly servant is being disrespectful—surely there was jealousy involved, too—and she begins mistreating her handmaid so badly that Hagar flees toward the city of Shur. Beside a spring in the wilderness, she encounters

the angel of the Lord, who instructs her to return to Sarah and submit to her, and not to despair because God promises that her son, too, will be the first of a multitude of descendants. The angel tells Hagar to name her son Ishmael, meaning "God hears," and informs her that he will be "a wild ass of a man" in near constant conflict with all his kin but the founder of a great people.

So she returns, gives birth to Ishmael, and endures Sarah's enmity until the child is 14. Eventually, Sarah gives birth to Isaac. When Sarah sees Ishmael playing with Isaac—some translations suggest Ishmael was mocking the infant—she is determined to send Hagar and Ishmael away. Once again, Hagar is cast into the wilderness. The scene that follows is heartrending: "When the water in the skin was gone, she cast the child under one of the bushes. Then she went and sat down opposite him a good way off, about the distance of a bow-shot; for she said, 'Do not let me look on the death of the child.' And as she sat opposite him, she lifted up her voice and wept." But as it was on Hagar's earlier journey to Shur, God hears her voice and opens her eyes and, lo and behold, there is a well filled with refreshing water nearby. And the angel of God speaks to her from heaven, "Come, lift up the boy and hold him fast with your hand, for I will make a great nation of him."

"So after Abram had lived 10 years in the land of Canaan, Sarai, Abram's wife, took Hagar the Egyptian, her slave-girl, and gave her to her husband Abram as a wife. He went into Hagar and she conceived...."

GENESIS 16:3

An angel of the Lord saved Hagar and Ishmael after Sarah cast Hagar out of Abraham's household.

23

Rebecca's compassion in giving a drink from the well to Abraham's servant marked her as Isaac's future wife.

Rebecca

Female Force

Wily and resourceful, she often takes matters into her own hands

ebecca is most assuredly one of the strongest female characters in the Bible. We first encounter her striding toward a well in her hometown of Nahor. Abraham has sent his servant back from Canaan to Abraham's native country to seek a bride for his son Isaac. When the servant reaches the well, he watches the young women approach to draw water in the gathering dusk; he prays to the Lord that whichever woman gives him water to drink and provides water for his camels be the wife he is seeking for Isaac. Then, "before he had finished speaking, there was Rebecca…coming out with her water jar on her shoulder. The girl was very fair to look upon, a virgin

whom no man has known." Sure enough, as the servant had hoped, Rebecca offers him a drink and then runs back to the well to draw enough water for his camels. She brings the servant to her household, where he meets her brother, the crafty Laban (see the story of Leah, page 30), who surely perked up when he beheld the many treasures the servant brought with him, including a gold nose-ring and two gold bracelets that he had already given Rebecca. Soon the deal is consummated—the servant bestows riches on one and all—and Laban agrees to allow Rebecca to travel with the servant to Canaan to become Isaac's wife. But one important detail remains: Rebecca must agree to the arrangement

Abraham's servant
presented Rebecca
with two golden
bracelets and a
nose-ring in thanks.

> *"'Drink, my Lord,' she said,*
> *and quickly lowered her jar upon*
> *her hand and gave him a drink.*
> *When she had finished giving him*
> *a drink, she said, 'I will draw*
> *for your camels also....'"*
>
> ### GENESIS 24:18–19

herself, just the first example of Rebecca taking matters into her own hands. Isaac, on the other hand, has no choice in the matter—as the bride was selected by his father, he must agree. Fortunately, he falls instantly in love with her and the marriage is an extremely happy one.

Next we encounter Rebecca as a mother-to-be. Having waited a long period of time to become pregnant, she is suffering through a difficult pregnancy with twins, who seem to be constantly at war with each other in her womb. Again, she takes the initiative, asking the Lord why she is suffering so. "Two nations are in your womb," the Lord tells her, "and two people born of you shall be divided; the one shall be stronger than the other, the elder shall serve the younger." And indeed, Esau, the first-born—hairy, impulsive, even foolish—ends up far less successful than his thoughtful, studious, introspective brother Jacob.

Rebecca's final, crowning act of independence is the ruse she perpetrates on an ailing, near-blind Isaac. Sensing that he is near death, Isaac calls Esau to him, preparing to bestow upon him the blessing that is Esau's due as the first born. But first, Isaac tells him to go to the fields and hunt for the game with which to prepare a meal to celebrate the blessing. Rebecca hears this exchange and immediately recruits

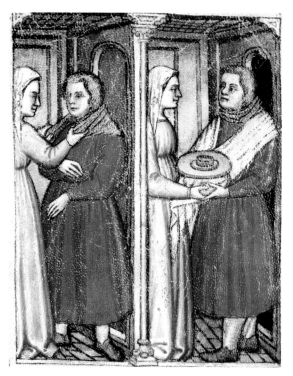

Rebecca's ruse included putting animal skins around Jacob's neck (above) and sending him in to a blind Isaac (right) with the feast Isaac had requested from Esau.

Jacob into her scheme to steal the blessing for her favored son. While Esau is out hunting, she prepares the savory meal herself, then dresses Isaac in Esau's clothes—including animal skins on his neck and hands to approximate the hairier Esau. The trick works: Isaac gives his blessing to Jacob, and Esau is furious. Rebecca may have perpetrated the hoax simply because she favored Jacob—she certainly did favor him—but she also surely knew that the blessing would determine the future leader of Isaac's clan and there was no question that Jacob was infinitely more suited for that role than Esau.

Finally, the resourceful Rebecca, the driver of the story from start to finish, directs Jacob to flee from Esau's wrath to her brother Laban's farm.

"Then Rebekah took the best garments of her elder son, Esau…and put them on her younger son, Jacob….Then she handed the savory food, and the bread she had prepared, to her son Jacob."

GENESIS 27:15 & 17

Though she didn't have the physical allure of her sister, Leah had a great inner beauty that the Lord recognized.

Faithful but Unloved

Her loveless marriage is salvaged by her bond with her children

The story of Leah is a tale of decidedly mixed blessings. Jacob, the son of Isaac, flees from the wrath of his brother Esau, who is incensed about Jacob's trickery in acquiring the birthright Esau considers rightfully his from their dying father, Isaac. Jacob's mother, Rebecca, tells Esau to go to her brother Laban's farm in Haran. As he nears the farm, he sees a beautiful woman leading a flock of sheep to a well and falls instantly in love with her. When he arrives at his uncle's farm, he learns that the woman at the well is Leah's younger sister, Rachel. Soon thereafter, he asks Laban if he can marry her—the selfish and crafty patriarch replies that he may, but only after Jacob completes seven years of work, assisting Laban to manage his farm and grow the business. Jacob performs his duties faithfully and Laban prospers, but at the end of seven years, on the eve of Jacob's wedding and under the cover of darkness, Laban sends Leah to Jacob's bed instead of Rachel. The next morning, when he discovers the ruse, the faithful Jacob agrees to marry Leah and undergo

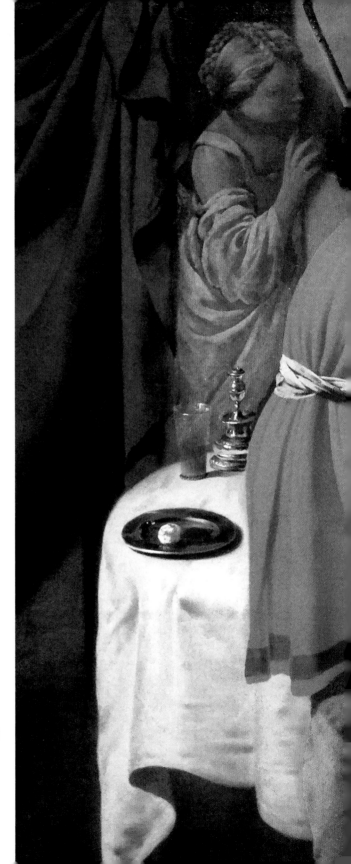

> *"Now Laban had two daughters; the name of the elder was Leah, and the name of the younger was Rachel. Leah's eyes were lovely, and Rachel was graceful and beautiful."*
>
> **GENESIS 29:16–17**

another seven years of service to Laban in exchange for the hand of Rachel.

Thus begins the marriage of Leah, who will be in love for the rest of her life with a man who does not return her affections. There is no indication that Jacob ever mistreats her, but her hope that her husband would come to love her goes unfulfilled. Her joy is limited to her role as mother, because while an envious Rachel struggles to conceive, Leah gives birth to six sons, who will found six of the 12 tribes of Israel. In introducing Leah, the Bible describes her eyes as "lovely" or, according to other translations, "weak" or "tender." Perhaps she was all those things, depending on the beholder. But in the generations to come, she would be remembered as one of the founding mothers of the nation of Israel.

Laban (seated) forces Jacob to accept Leah, in blue, as Jacob's first wife.

33

Rachel

Favored Wife

The one Jacob loves, she eventually gives birth to Joseph, the next great patriarch

achel's tale is the flip side of Leah's. The Bible describes her as "graceful and beautiful" and Jacob is smitten with her from the moment he sees her bringing her flock to the well to be watered. We are never told whether she loves Jacob; perhaps he is doomed, like his wife, Leah, to love someone who will never love him back. We know that she envies her sister, to whom God grants the gift of children in compensation for the lack of love she experiences from her husband. And we know that in the end God hears her plea and "opens her womb," enabling her to give birth to two sons, one of whom, Joseph, will become the next key player in the drama of the chosen people after

the death of his father, Jacob. Later in the narrative, she plays the trickster—the Bible presents many of these—by stealing Laban's "household gods" during Jacob's hurried departure from Laban's farm. Scholars suggest that these were probably statues representing ancestral gods and establishing Laban's authority within the family as well as legitimating his property claims. Finding them missing and Jacob gone, Laban pursues him and his large entourage. When he catches up to his son-in-law, though, a thorough search of his camp fails to turn up any of the household gods, leading Jacob to criticize Laban harshly for chasing after him so aggressively. What Jacob does not know is that Rachel was the thief,

Jacob fell in love with
Rachel from his first sight
of her at the well.

and that when Laban and his men entered her tent to search for the missing goods, she was sitting on them, telling Laban that she was unable to get up because she was menstruating. "Let not my lord be angry that I cannot rise before you," she tells her father, "for the way of women is upon me."

She is beautiful, she is envious, and she is devious—some interpreters have connected these adjectives to suggest that Rachel is the Bible's version of a "material girl," selfish and only concerned about her own standing. But in truth, the Bible only tells us that she sometimes gave in to such impulses, not that they constituted the whole of her character.

Household gods, embodied in figures like this, were important tokens of family status.

According to strict Jewish law, anything menstruating women touch is unclean. Rachel used that to hide her theft, sitting atop the stolen goods so her father couldn't search for them.

"*And when Rachel saw that she bare Jacob no children, Rachel envied her sister; and said unto Jacob, 'Give me children, or else I die.'*"

GENESIS 30:1

37

> "But the midwives feared God; they did not do as the king of Egypt commanded them, but they let the boys live.... So the king of Egypt summoned the midwives and said to them, 'Why have you done this, and allowed the boys to live?'"
>
> *EXODUS 1:17-18*

The midwives used their wits to deceive the Pharaoh and defy his deadly decree.

Shiphrah and Puah

Courageous Midwives

Two women who boldly disobeyed the Pharaoh thwarted the genocide of Jewish children

pon the death of the kindly Pharaoh who reigned during Joseph's time, Egypt became subjected to a new, brutish king with a harsh attitude toward the Hebrews. Feeling threatened by the prosperous, expanding Jewish population in Egypt, the ruler feared he might be deposed by one of them—so he devised a nefarious plan of genocide in hopes of shoring up his own power. Fortunately, the midwives Shiphrah and Puah were able to undermine its execution.

In Exodus chapter 1, we are told that the Pharaoh summoned Shiphrah and Puah to the palace and commanded them to execute all male Hebrew babies at birth. "When you act as midwives to the Hebrew women, and see them on the birthstool, if it is a boy, kill him; but if it is a girl, she shall live," the Pharaoh instructed.

Being God-fearing believers, Shiphrah and Puah (who historians say may have been the top midwives in charge of hundreds of others) refuse to carry out the Pharaoh's decree, thereby allowing a spate of Hebrew male births. When the Pharaoh demands an explanation for their disobedience, the women shrewdly defer to biology: They insist that because the Hebrews were so vigorous, their labor was shorter than that of Egyptian women—and therefore the babies had been born before the midwives arrived.

The Pharaoh would go on to issue other murderous decrees in his bid to decimate the Hebrews. But because of these two courageous midwives, many male newborns were spared—one of whom was likely Moses, the future spiritual leader and most important prophet in Judaism. As a reward for their actions, God blessed both Shiphrah and Puah with their own extensive families and a long line of descendants who would become the dynastic Levite priesthood.

> *"The woman conceived and bore a son; and when she saw that he was a fine baby, she hid him for three months. When she could hide him no longer, she got a papyrus basket for him, and plastered it with bitumen and pitch; she put the child in it and placed it among the reeds on the bank of the river."*
>
> EXODUS 2:2-3

Jochebed's courage, cleverness and trust in the Lord earned her a prominent place among the heroines of the Bible.

Jochebed

Mother of Moses

Hoping for a miracle, she set her baby adrift in a basket, holding faith that God had a plan for him

Behind only the Virgin Mary, Jochebed may be the most important mother in all of the Bible, yet we know little about her. As the mother of Moses, she made a deep personal sacrifice that would impact the Israelites for centuries to come: She gave up her son to save his life.

With the worst possible timing, Jochebed delivers her son in Egypt during the Pharaoh's reign of terror over the Jews. The ruler had attempted to have all newborn Hebrew boys murdered by midwives, but thanks to the intervention of Shiphrah and Puah, babies like Moses survived. Frustrated and enraged, the Pharaoh then decrees that all male Hebrew babies should be cast into the Nile and drowned—a law that was carried out with a vengeance.

Jochebed sees that her son is healthy and strong, but she is terrified for his safety. She keeps him hidden at home for three months, but eventually the boy's cries grow too loud and she can no longer conceal his presence. In an act of desperation, Jochebed prepares a papyrus basket, seals it with tar and pitch so it will float, and places baby Moses inside it. Hoping for a miracle, she then places the little basket among the bulrushes along the banks of the Nile and sets it adrift. She must have

suffered unimaginable pain as she abandoned her baby, but God had a divine plan in which she was playing a faithful role.

Later, the Pharaoh's daughter comes to a spot along the Nile to bathe and notices the small basket wedged among the reeds. She asks her maid to retrieve it, and when she peered inside, "she found the baby boy…he was crying, and her heart melted with compassion." All the while, Miriam, Moses' older sister, is watching from a hiding place—and as the scene unfolds, she approaches, volunteering to find a "Hebrew woman" to nurse the baby. The Pharaoh's daughter agrees, despite knowing that such boys were to be drowned, and even offers to pay a nurse for her trouble. Miriam runs and fetches Jochebed, the baby's true mother, who is hired as a wet nurse. Destined for greatness, Moses goes on to be adopted by the Pharaoh's daughter and is raised in the palace among Egyptian royalty. Although it must have caused her great anguish to keep her maternal secret, Jochebed produced, in her three children—Moses, Miriam and their brother, Aaron—a crucial trio of leaders who would, with God's guidance, usher the Israelites out of Egypt into their destiny in the promised land.

Miriam led the women of Israel in a joyous celebration after their escape from Egypt.

Miriam
Leading Woman

The sister of Moses is part of his story from the very beginning

Miriam played a pivotal role in the liberation of the Hebrew people from captivity in Egypt and, along with her brothers, Moses and Aaron, becomes one of the three most influential leaders of the Israelites as they trek through the wilderness in search of the promised land. We first learn of her, though her name is not mentioned, soon after the birth of Moses, when the Pharaoh—the ruler of Egypt—decrees that all male babies of Hebrew descent are to be thrown into the Nile and drowned. Desperate to save her child, Moses' mother fashions a papyrus basket for him, plasters it "with bitumen and pitch," and places the baby in a basket that she leaves in the reeds at the edge of the river. Miriam stands guard over her brother from a distance, protecting him from danger, until the Pharaoh's daughter finds

the baby and adopts Moses as her own, though she allows Moses' mother to be the child's wet nurse.

Miriam next makes an appearance after God parts the Red Sea to enable the Israelites to escape the Egyptians, "the waters forming a wall for them on their right and on their left," while their pursuers are thrown into the sea and drowned, just as the Pharaoh had drowned so many Hebrew babies for so many years. Miriam, now the unofficial leader of the Israelite women and identified as a prophet herself, leads an impromptu celebration: "Then the prophet Miriam, Aaron's sister, took a tambourine in her hand; and all the women went out after her with tambourines and with dancing. And Miriam sang to them: 'Sing to the Lord, for he has triumphed gloriously; horse and rider he has thrown into the sea.'"

Confident that God would protect them after they left Egypt, Miriam and the other Israeli women took musical instruments with them to praise him.

> *"And Miriam sang to them: 'Sing to the Lord, for he has triumphed gloriously; horse and rider he has thrown into sea.'"*
>
> *EXODUS 15:21*

Later, as the Israelites suffer a host of privations in the wilderness and start to grumble about Moses' leadership, Miriam and Aaron also begin to question Moses' preeminent position. First, they criticize Moses' marriage to a "Cushite" woman, presumably Zipporah, a reflection of the Israelites' disapproval of unions with foreigners. Next they question Moses' special relationship with God: "Has the Lord only spoken through Moses? Has he not spoken through us also?" God sternly sets them straight, noting that he speaks to other prophets in visions and dreams, but with Moses, "I speak face to face—clearly, not in riddles, and he beholds the form of the Lord." For her insubordination, Miriam is struck with leprosy—a term that referred to a variety of skin ailments in the ancient world—and is banished from the Israelite camp for seven days, after which she is healed and allowed to return, presumably performing faithful service to the Lord for the rest of her days.

The Bible reports that Miriam, after many years of wandering with her people, died in the wilderness of Zin, in a waterless place called Kadesh. After Miriam's death, the Israelites complain of the lack of water and, at God's direction, Moses strikes a rock twice and produces a copious flow of water for all. Water is everywhere in the story of Miriam, from the Nile to the Red Sea to the water from the rock.

Zipporah

To the Rescue

The foreign-born wife of Moses saves her husband's life

Zipporah makes only two brief appearances in the Bible. The first is when she encounters Moses at the well near her home in Midian. (The theme of a well as the place where significant meetings take place recurs throughout both the Old and New Testaments.) She and a group of women are prevented from watering their sheep by an apparently obstreperous group of shepherds. Moses drives the shepherds away and helps the women to complete their task. When Zipporah returns home, she recounts the story of Moses' intervention, and her father, a priest, tells her to invite him to dinner. Zipporah is one of seven daughters, and soon she and Moses are married, with her father's blessing.

Her second brief appearance comes later, as Moses is returning from Midian to Egypt, where he will begin his critical confrontation with the Pharaoh. In a strange passage, the Bible tells us that "the Lord tried to kill" Moses; Zipporah then circumcises her son—a ritual requirement that should have already been performed—and touches Moses' feet (a euphemism for genitals) with the boy's foreskin, and Moses is spared. Scholars disagree about the precise meaning of this unusual anecdote, but one point is clear: Moses is saved yet again, as he was as a baby, by a woman.

> *"Moses agreed to stay with the man, and he gave Moses his daughter Zipporah in marriage. She bore a son, and he named him Gershom; for he said, 'I have been an alien residing in a foreign land.'"*
>
> EXODUS 2:21–22

After helping Zipporah at the well, Moses married her, though the wedding ceremony picture above is not described in the Bible.

"Moses brought their case before the Lord. And the Lord spoke to Moses, saying: "The daughters of Zelophehad are right in what they are saying. You shall indeed . . . pass the inheritance of their father on to them."

NUMBERS 27:7

The five sisters boldly made their plea to Moses before a crowd of mostly men.

Mahlah, Noa, Hoglah, Milcah and Tirzah

The Daughters of Zelophehad

Five daughters stand up for their rights and establish them forever

The daughters of Zelophehad appear only briefly, but they have a big impact. As the Israelites are camped near Jericho, poised to enter the Promised Land, Moses orders that a census be taken of all the tribes of Israel, in part to determine the rules for the apportionment of land in the soon-to-be nation. The total population—apparently of adults—is 601,730. Among that number, the Bible tells us, only Caleb and Joshua— soon to become Israel's great military leader—remain among the people who were counted many years before in the Sinai wilderness. At the conclusion of the census, as Moses is promulgating the laws that God has given him for the division of land, Zelophehad's daughters step forward—an act of great bravery in their male-dominated culture—and petition Moses, saying: "Our father died in the wilderness...and he had no sons. Why should the name of our father be taken away from his clan because he had no son? Give to us a possession among our father's brothers." So Moses takes the matter to God, who tells him, "The daughters of Zelophehad are right in what they are saying; you shall indeed let them possess an inheritance among their father's brothers." This divine proclamation established the right of women to inherit property.

"*Then the king of Jericho sent orders to Rahab, 'Bring out the men who have come to you, who entered your house, for they have come only to search out the whole land.' But the woman took the two men and hid them.*"

JOSHUA 2:3–4

Rahab endangered her own life by providing the Israelites' first safe house in the promised land.

Rahab

Redemption and Reward

A Jericho woman shelters Israelite spies, paving the way for Joshua's first victory in Canaan

During the lead-up to the decisive battle of Jericho, the Israelites found an unlikely ally in Rahab, a former harlot whose belief in God led her to defy her own king. The battle of Jericho was destined to be the first the Israelites would fight in their conquest of Canaan, and as they prepared to cross the river Jordan, two spies were sent into Jericho to observe what conditions awaited them.

When the king of Jericho catches wind of the presence of foreign operatives, he launches a citywide search for them. In a gutsy move, Rahab shelters them in her home in Jericho, hiding them on her roof beneath piles of reeds. The soldiers come knocking, but Rahab stands her ground, insisting that the spies had been there earlier, but had since left the city.

While her deception would surely have meant death if discovered, Rahab had nurtured a growing faith in God since she'd first heard of the Hebrews' miraculous escape from Egypt via the parting of the Red Sea about 40 years earlier. The Book of Joshua quotes her as telling the spies, "I know that the Lord has given you this land and that a great fear of you has fallen on us…so that all who live in this country are melting in fear because of you." In return for her protection, the grateful spies vow to spare Rahab and her family once the battle of Jericho begins. She is told to mark her house—which was built into the city wall—by hanging a long scarlet rope out of a window as a signal to the Israelite soldiers not to harm her and her relatives.

When the spies return to the Israelite encampment, their positive report provides the necessary encouragement for Joshua, who had succeeded Moses as leader, to launch one of the strangest battles in military history. At God's instruction, Joshua leads his army in marching around the entire city of Jericho once each day for six days, blowing their trumpets as they do. By the seventh day, with the population of the city quaking in fear, the troops march around the wall seven times, then let out a great shout. At that moment the walls fall, allowing the city to be invaded and conquered. We're told that by God's order every living thing was to be destroyed—except for Rahab and her family.

Although she would forever be remembered as a harlot, Rahab is a gritty heroine and a symbol of God's grace and redemptive powers, which extend even to Gentiles and former sinners. Because she risked her life to serve God, the Israelites were able to establish a foothold in the Promised Land. In the New Testament, we learn that God rewarded Rahab by making her one of Jesus' ancestors. She is named in Matthew's genealogy of Christ as the mother of Boaz and great-grandmother of King David.

Deborah

Prophet and Warrior

Very few leaders filled as many roles as this dynamic figure

The biblical Book of Judges recounts a period of great instability for the people of Israel, who, lacking solid leadership, continued to disobey God's commandments and so are delivered by God into the hands of a line of oppressive foreign powers. The judges—best understood as "rulers"—were a series of charismatic leaders who stepped into the breach, returning the people to righteousness and peace, but ultimately leaving the land in chaos again after their deaths. Among the most fascinating of these is Deborah, who rose to power in a male-dominated society by dint of her powerful connection to God as one of the few female prophets.

Deborah regularly dispensed justice and governed the affairs of the Israelites from her favored location beneath a rare palm tree in the "hill country of Ephraim." The people were then under the yoke of King Jabin of Canaan, who had controlled their lands and oppressed them for some 20 years. The people "cried out to the Lord for help." Deborah summons a soldier named Barak and presents him with God's command that he recruit a force of 10,000 men to fight the army of Sisera, King Jabin's mighty military leader. Barak agrees, but only if Deborah will go into battle with him. And so Deborah the prophet and leader becomes Deborah the warrior, leading the army against a much larger Canaanite force and winning a great victory after the "Lord threw Sisera and all his chariots and all his army into a panic." The Bible concludes the narrative this way: "So perish all your enemies, O Lord! But may your friends be like the sun as it rises in its might....And the land had rest 40 years."

Deborah judged the people of Israel and later led them into battle against the Canaanites.

"And she said, 'I will surely go with you; nevertheless, the road on which you are going will not lead to your glory for the Lord will deliver Sisera into the hands of a woman.'"

JUDGES 4:9

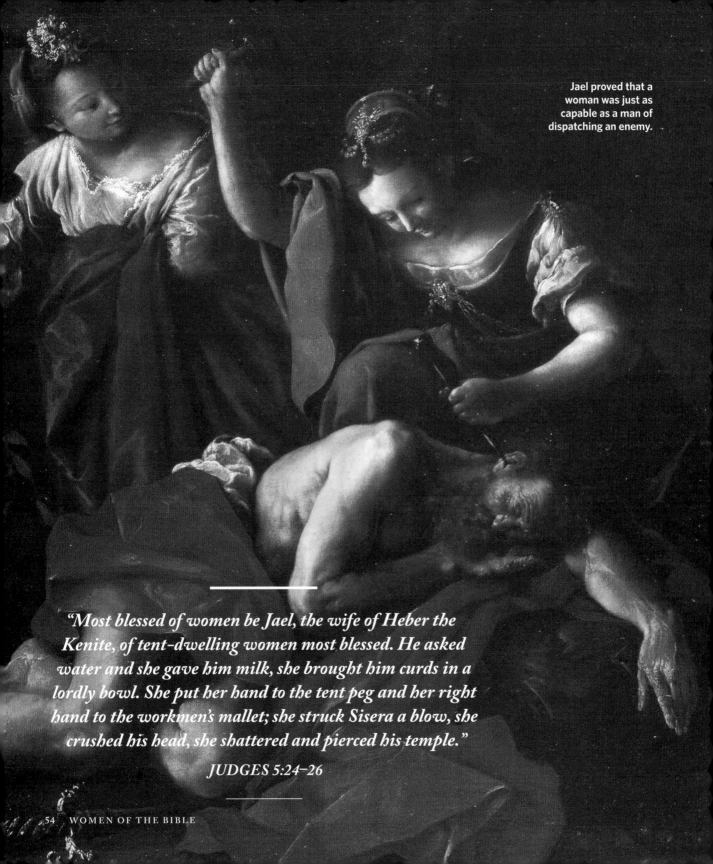

Jael proved that a woman was just as capable as a man of dispatching an enemy.

"Most blessed of women be Jael, the wife of Heber the Kenite, of tent-dwelling women most blessed. He asked water and she gave him milk, she brought him curds in a lordly bowl. She put her hand to the tent peg and her right hand to the workmen's mallet; she struck Sisera a blow, she crushed his head, she shattered and pierced his temple."

JUDGES 5:24–26

Jael

Fierce Assassin

Her cold-blooded killing of an enemy commander turns the tide in favor of God's people

To understand the importance of Jael, some historical context is helpful. It is the time of Deborah, the notorious prophetess and judge, and the Hebrews are at war with the Canaanites, fighting to claim the land of "milk and honey" that God had promised them. Leading the enemy armies is Sisera, a vicious warlord who had oppressed the Israelites for 20 years. From a stronghold on Mount Tabor, Deborah—along with her top general, Barak, and his army—is able to launch a tide-turning battle in which they swiftly overrun Sisera's army. In the book of Judges, we're told that Sisera, in one last-ditch effort to save his life, gets out of his chariot and flees on foot into the plains where nomads are encamped.

That's where he encounters Jael, a fearless Bedouin sympathetic to the Israelites. Luring the unsuspecting Sisera into her tent for refuge, she lulls him into a false sense of security, providing him food and a rug to hide beneath. When he requests water, Jael brings him milk, perhaps to make him sleepy. At peace, Sisera drifts off—and Jael swings into action using the only tools she has at hand: a spike and a mallet. According to Judges 5:21, Jael "took a tent peg, and took a hammer in her hand, and went softly to him and drove the peg into his temple, until it went down into the ground—he was lying fast asleep from weariness—and he died."

The killing fulfills Deborah's prophecy to Barak that the Lord would "deliver Sisera into the hands of a woman." Remarkably, Jael chose to assassinate Sisera without seeking approval from her husband or any other male figureheads in the community. When the time came, she didn't hesitate: She realized that soon Sisera would be awake again, and she seized the moment to do what God was asking her to do. She had no swords or other weapons—hers was a woman's tent. But as a Bedouin, she was skilled at driving tent spikes and she used what she knew. The grisly killing didn't single-handedly win the war, but it was the beginning of the end for the Canaanites' rule of Israel.

Ruth (at left) showed great love and loyalty for her daughters-in-law Naomi and Orpah.

Ruth & Naomi

A Love Story

Loyalty and compassion stand at the center of their tale

> *"So she said, 'See, your sister-in-law has*
> *gone back to her people and her gods;*
> *return after your sister-in law.' But Ruth*
> *said, 'Do not press me to leave you…'"*
>
> *RUTH 1:15–16*

The stories of Ruth and Naomi cannot be told separately because their relationship, among the most poignant in the entire Bible, stands at the center of the narrative. Their story begins in tragedy: Naomi's husband and her two sons die, making widows of Naomi and her two daughters-in-law, Ruth and Orpah. Decimated by her loss and convinced that the Lord has turned against her, Naomi decides to return from the country of Moab to Bethlehem in her homeland. Orpah and Ruth begin the journey with her, but soon after setting out, Naomi urges them to return to Moab, arguing that she is too old to give birth to additional sons to marry them, and even if she could conceive, would Orpah and Ruth wait until they were grown? She must also have had in her mind the fact that Moabites were not viewed favorably by her people, and the two younger women were likely to face discrimination back in Judah. Orpah agrees and reluctantly turns back, but Ruth refuses, clinging to Naomi and entreating her:

"Do not press me to leave you
   or to turn back from following you!
Where you go, I will go;
   where you lodge, I will lodge;
your people shall be my people,

and your God my God.
Where you die, I will die—
there I will be buried.
May the Lord do thus and so to me,
   and more as well,
if even death parts me from you!"

And so loyal and loving Ruth remains with her mother-in-law and travels to a strange land where she knows no one. It is a breathtaking leap of faith, for which she is wonderfully rewarded when she comes to the attention of a rich landowner named Boaz, who takes an immediate interest in her. When she appears in his fields to "glean among the ears of grain," Boaz tells his men to allow her to take what she needs and not to bother her. When Ruth asks him why he is being so kind to a foreigner, Boaz praises her for her kindness to her mother-in-law and for leaving her own father and mother and her native land to care for her. "May the Lord reward you for your deeds," he declares, "and may you have a full reward from the Lord, the God of Israel, under whose wings you have come for refuge!"

Wise Naomi, sensing Boaz's interest in Ruth and knowing that he is in fact a kinsman of hers—a role that requires him to protect her—conspires to bring the two together. She directs Ruth to dress

Ruth clung to Naomi
and begged to
accompany her
to Naomi's former
home in Bethlehem.

59

> *"Then Boaz said to Ruth, 'Now listen, my daughter, do not go to glean in another field or leave this one, but keep close to my young women....I have ordered the young men not to bother you.'"*
>
> RUTH 3:8–9

The tending of fields like this one is a major theme in the tale of Ruth and Naomi.

in her finest attire and go to the threshing floor in the evening, after Boaz, happy and content, has eaten and drank and lies down to sleep. She is to lift the cover off his feet and lie down herself beside them. She does as she is told, and at midnight Boaz awakes to find Ruth lying at his feet. Unsure who she is in the darkness, she tells him, "I am Ruth, your servant, spread your cloak over your servant, for you are next-of-kin." Boaz is touched by her gesture and her loyalty to the ties of kinship. Soon the pair is married and Ruth gives birth to a son, whom Naomi will love and serve as nurse. "He shall be to you a restorer of life and a nourisher of your old age; for your daughter-in-law who loves you, who is more to you than seven sons, has borne him." The son's name was Obed, who became the father of Jesse, who became the father of David, the great king of Israel, and an ancestor of Jesus of Nazareth. And so a tale of extraordinary compassion and generosity, with a non-Israelite at its center, becomes the foundation of a family of vast importance to Christians and Jews alike.

"*When Delilah realized that he had told her his whole secret, she sent and called the lords of the Philistines, saying, 'This time come up, for he has told his whole secret to me.'*"

JUDGES 16:18

Once Delilah knew the hidden source of Samson's strength, he was doomed.

Delilah
Samson's Betrayer

Samson is undone by love and the wiles of a beautiful woman

The women in the Bible exemplify a variety of virtues: strength, wisdom, modesty, compassion, faithfulness to God's will—and sometimes a combination of all the above. But the Bible also includes a bona fide female villain, and her name is Delilah. Some claim that she was a Philistine, but the Bible tells us nothing of her ethnicity; others say she was a prostitute, but the scriptures give us no indication of that, either. What we do know is that she began a passionate relationship with Samson, one of the Israelite judges, like Deborah. He was dealing with a different oppressor: Deborah challenged the might of the Canaanites; Samson fought the Philistines. Like the Greek figure of Hercules, Samson was legendary for his exceptional strength, as displayed in a series of superhuman feats. Alas, Samson's physical strength was not matched by strong moral character or acute intelligence. Before he even met Delilah, he had shown decidedly poor judgment in his involvement with women.

Samson apparently dallied with many women, including prostitutes, but the Bible reports that he fell in love with Delilah, and it was that devotion to a woman who clearly did not reciprocate his feelings that led to his downfall. Did Delilah seduce Samson with the intent of betraying him? That is not clear, but once the Philistines come calling with the offer of several thousand pieces of silver—a small fortune— she gladly accepts the assignment to destroy her lover. Three times she asks Samson to tell her the source of his exceptional strength; three times he gives her answers that prove bogus when the Philistines arrive to capture him. Finally, the Bible reports that "after she had nagged him with her words day after day, and pestered him, he was tired to death." So he tells her that if he is deprived of his magnificent mane of hair—which had never been cut, in keeping with his vow as a Nazirite dedicated to God—he would lose his strength and be as other men.

Delilah promptly calls in a barber to shear Samson's locks while he is sleeping, and Samson is then unable to fight back when the Philistines arrive to seize him and gouge out his eyes. But Samson has one final heroic act to perform: When the Philistines bring him to their celebratory party—"Our god has given our enemy into our hand!"—to mock him and laugh at his infirmity, Samson, having begged God for a last burst of strength, is able to pull down the pillars of the house in which the Philistine lords are gathered, killing them all but losing his own life in the process. The Bible does not report how Delilah spent the fortune she received in exchange for her treachery.

Hannah

Answered Prayer

A desperate temple visit leads to the birth of one of Israel's greatest prophets

Hannah is one of several biblical women who beseeched God for relief from their apparent inability to conceive a child, a reflection of how important childbearing was to the identity and status of women in the ancient world. Hannah's pain is exacerbated by the fact that Peninnah, the other wife of her husband, Elkanah, has been able to have children, while Hannah has remained barren. In despair, she goes to the temple and prays to God for relief, promising that if God will grant her a son, she will dedicate him to God as "a Nazirite until the day of his death. He shall drink neither wine nor intoxicants, and no razor shall touch his head." Eli, the high priest, observing her weeping and noting that her lips were moving but no words were discernible, believes her to be drunk, but when Hannah explains her plight—"I have been pouring out my soul before the Lord"—he tells her: "Go in peace; the God of Israel grant the petition you have made to him." And so Hannah, once without child, gives birth to a son whom she names Samuel, meaning "heard by God." Later, she brings the boy to Eli, reminds him of their earlier meeting, and tells him: "I have lent him [Samuel] to the Lord; as long as he lives he is given to the Lord." Samuel, conceived through his mother's devotion to God, would go on to become one of the great prophets and leaders of Israel.

Hannah's devotion to her faith eventually gave Israel one of its greatest leaders.

"And the Lord took note of Hannah; she conceived and bore three sons and two daughters. And the boy Samuel grew up in the presence of the Lord."

SAMUEL 2:21

Bathsheba

Sin and Redemption

Lust led to transgression, but God's forgiveness saves the day

King David, the beloved and charismatic leader of the Israelites, is strolling on the roof of his palace one evening when he spies a beautiful woman—"very beautiful," according to the biblical account—bathing in one of the homes below. Kings were as powerful then as they have been throughout history, so it was no difficult matter for David to demand that the woman be brought to him. And when he asks her to lie down with him—the Bible does not report the nature of the request—it is not surprising that she would acquiesce. Perhaps she was as filled with desire as he was, or maybe she felt powerless to resist, fearing the consequences were she to say no. Before she arrives, David learns that her name is Bathsheba, and that she is married to a Hittite man named Uriah.

Later, when David discovers that Bathsheba is pregnant, he compounds the sin of adultery by attempting to cover his crime. First, he has Uriah brought back from battle in hopes that he would have sex with his wife, thereby making the world believe that the baby on the way was fathered by Bathsheba's husband rather than by the philandering king. Then, when Uriah refuses to sleep with his wife while his fellow soldiers are in

jeopardy at the front, David sends a note via Uriah to his commander on the battlefield: "Set Uriah in the forefront of the fighting, and then draw back from him, so that he may be struck down and die."

These transgressions of the king, who would become known as the founder of Israel, were grievous indeed. Nathan—one in a long line of Israelite prophets, honored and protected even when they directly challenged the power of the ruling authorities—was unstinting in his condemnation of David's behavior: "Why have you despised the word of the Lord, to do what is evil in his sight?"

The child that was conceived in sin lives only seven days, despite David's pleas to God to spare his newborn son. But David humbly acknowledges his iniquity—the Bible reports it as the only blot on his long record of faithful service to God—and consoles Bathsheba, whom he marries soon after Uriah's death. And the next child born to the couple is Solomon, who would become revered for his wise stewardship of the nation of Israel. In Solomon, the sin of the father was redeemed. And Bathsheba, as the mother of Solomon, would be mentioned in Matthew's chronicle of the genealogy of Jesus many centuries later.

As Bathsheba was bathing, David watched her from high above. "So David sent messengers to get her," the Bible reports, "and she came to him...."

"He saw from the roof a woman bathing and she was very beautiful. David sent someone to inquire about the woman. It was reported, 'This is Bathsheba, daughter of Eliam, the wife of Uriah the Hittite.'"

2 SAMUEL 11:2–3

"No, my brother, do not force me; for such a thing is not done in Israel; do not do anything so vile! As for me, where could I carry my shame?"

2 SAMUEL 13:12–13

Tamar strongly objected, but Amnon raped her anyway, then callously discarded her.

Tamar

Beauty Defiled

A shocking rape ruins a life and leads to years of conflict in Israel

In the midst of inspirational stories about women who wield influence despite the male-dominated society in which they live, the Bible gives us the tragic saga of Tamar, a woman whose powerlessness stands as a rebuke to anyone tempted to understate the difficult road faced by women in ancient society. The daughter of King David, she is considered unusually attractive even among David's many good-looking offspring. In Tamar's case, however, her beauty is a curse, because her half-brother Amnon becomes obsessed with her. "Amnon was so tormented that he made himself ill because of his sister Tamar, for she was a virgin and it seemed impossible to Amnon to do anything to her." He enlists the help of his "crafty" friend Jonadab, who concocts a scheme: First, Amnon feigns an illness that drives him to bed. When David comes to check on him, Amnon requests that Tamar bring him food. She appears in Amnon's rooms, presumably with her retinue. At first, Amnon petulantly refuses to eat, then orders all the servants to leave. Once settled in his bed, with Tamar feeding him by hand, Amnon "took hold of her, and said to her, 'Come lie with me, my sister.'" She refuses: "Do not do anything so vile! Where could I carry my shame?" She even tries

to convince Amnon that he could go to their father and ask for her as his wife. Such a union, while not entirely conventional, would nonetheless be accepted. But Amnon is not interested in being honorable: "Being stronger than she, he forced her and lay with her." Even after his violent assault, Amnon could have salvaged Tamar's reputation by marrying her, but he "was seized by a very great loathing for her; indeed, his loathing was even greater than the lust he had felt for her." And so he compounds the rape by ordering his servant to throw her out of his room. In agony, Tamar rips the robe she is wearing, pours ashes on her head, and goes away, "crying aloud as she went." Tamar's standing is ruined—no man will marry her and she is shunned. We know nothing more about her life except that, "Tamar remained, a desolate woman, in her brother Absalom's house."

David learns of the rape and is angry, but nothing is done to Amnon, and he goes unpunished for two years until Absalom, who harbors a deep hatred of his brother, engineers an opportunity to have him killed. Amnon's death and Absalom's subsequent flight lead to decades of strife, the ripples from Amnon's sin spreading ever wider in the years to come.

Jezebel's reign of terror finally ended when her eunuch servants threw her from the window.

"This is the word of the Lord, which he spoke by his servant Elijah the Tishite. 'The dogs shall eat the flesh of Jezebel; the corpse of Jezebel shall be like dung in the field....'"

2 KINGS 9:36–37

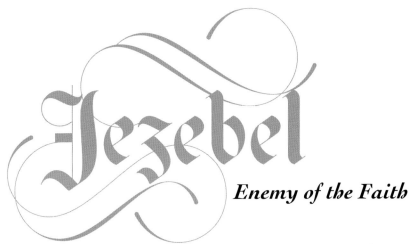

Jezebel

Enemy of the Faith

Her very name has come to represent selfishness and treachery

In Jezebel, we find a villain to rival and perhaps surpass Delilah. While Delilah betrays Samson, a single leader of Israel, Jezebel—fierce, ambitious, clever—seeks to destroy an entire religion and lead the people of Israel to worship the false gods of Baal, Ashtaroth and Astarte. She comes to power by marrying Ahab, the weak and faithless king of Northern Israel—the kingdom was divided into two parts at the time—despite her heritage as the daughter of Ethbaal, a king of Sidon and a Baal worshipper.

Her sins are plentiful: At her direction, many of the Hebrew priests are murdered or forced into hiding; when Naboth, a righteous worshipper of the Lord, refuses to sell his land to the king, Jezebel has false charges lodged against him that lead to his being stoned to death, thus freeing his property for the king to seize. She urges her husband to erect temples to Baal throughout the land and to worship the false idols himself. "Indeed, there was no one like Ahab," the Bible reports, "who sold himself to do what was evil in the sight of the Lord, urged on by his wife Jezebel."

In the end, both Ahab and Jezebel are destroyed by the faithful forces called into action by the prophet Elijah, who accurately predicts the duo's downfall. Jezebel is killed in a particularly gruesome manner: She is thrown from a window—"some of her blood spattered on the wall"—and trampled by horses. When soldiers are sent to bury her, "they found no more of her than the skull and the feet and the palms of her hands." Thus was dispatched one of the Bible's most hated women.

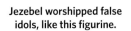

Jezebel worshipped false idols, like this figurine.

71

"*Now when Athaliah…saw that her son was dead, she set about to destroy all the royal family of the house of Judah. But Jehosheba, the king's daughter, took Joash, son of Ahaziah, and stole him away from among the king's children who were about to be killed.*"
2 CHRONICLES 22:10-11

Jehosheba hid her baby nephew, heir to the throne, before he could be killed.

Jehosheba

Heroic Aunt

A princess rescues a royal heir—and preserves the house of David

During the dark years following the ruthless reign of Jezebel and Ahab, the princess Jehosheba rose as a beacon of light whose courage would help heal the nation of Judah. As murder and mayhem swept the kingdom, a bloody massacre was ordered by Jezebel's daughter Athaliah to wipe out all the heirs to the throne of David. Some 40 members of the royal family were put to death so that she could claim the crown. But Jehosheba, aunt to the infant heir Joash, cleverly plucks her nephew out of harm's way. While the Bible doesn't spell out the details, scholars suggest that she steals him from the palace nursery (perhaps by replacing him with another child) and secures him and his nurse away from Athaliah's henchmen.

Conveniently, as the wife of the high priest, Jehosheba has access to the inner chambers of the temple where only holy men, such as her husband, are permitted. There, deep inside the temple walls, baby Joash, the sole survivor of the line of Judah, is nurtured in secret for six years. When the boy is 7 years old, Jehosheba and her husband stage a coup d'etat against Athaliah, and Joash is crowned and anointed king. He would reign for 40 years, during which time worship of Yahweh was restored in Judah. Most notably, with the brave act of rescuing her brother's son, Jehosheba saves the so-called "royal seed," thereby preserving God's promise that the Messiah would come to Earth through the lineage of David.

Huldah proved her mettle
as an authoritative woman
chosen by God to be His
interpreter and mouthpiece.

"So [they] went to the prophetess Huldah....
She declared to them... 'Thus
says the Lord, I will indeed bring
disaster on this place and on
its inhabitants—all the words of the
book that the king of Judah has read.
Because they have abandoned me and
have made offerings to other gods.'"

2 KINGS 22:14–17

Huldah

Teacher and Oracle

Through her influence and insight, she exemplifies the importance of listening for God's voice

As one of the seven female prophets (along with Sarah, Miriam, Deborah, Hannah, Abigail and Esther), Huldah played a crucial role in the great spiritual renaissance that occurred under King Josiah, who was considered Judah's last good king. Married to the keeper of the royal wardrobe, Huldah held high social rank in Jerusalem and was one of the inner circle of King Josiah. She was also related to the eminent prophet Jeremiah, both being descendants of Rahab, the former harlot who hid the Israelite spies in Jericho.

Through her definitive prophecies, Huldah relayed messages from God to the high priests and royal officials—and is also said to have publicly shared her visions at a place now called Huldah's Gate in Jerusalem. The Bible does not elaborate on all of her divinations, instead focusing mainly on

Huldah's most notable—and dire—prediction: the coming destruction of Judah.

Because the Jewish people had largely abandoned Yahweh for other gods and false idols, Huldah fearlessly foretold that God's "wrath had been kindled" and punishment was at hand. Only the king, Josiah, would be spared, due to his piety; he would die "in peace" before "the evil" would befall the people. Huldah's prophecies became reality, as the Israelites were soon overtaken by Egypt and then Babylon, inciting the Great Diaspora that scattered the Jews away from their homeland. We don't know Huldah's ultimate fate in life, but the prophetess stands in biblical history as a remarkable woman in a rare position of authority, one who boldly relayed the words of God and played a role that was on an equal basis with men.

The Talmud calls Abigail one of the "four women of surpassing beauty in the world."

"David said to Abigail....
May you be blessed for your good
judgment and for keeping me
from bloodshed this day.'"

1 SAMUEL 25:32-33

Abigail

Diplomat and Oracle

In a patriarchal society, she's a master of subtle negotiation

I n 1 Samuel 25, we meet Abigail, "an intelligent and beautiful woman" who is the wife of a wealthy but foolish man named Nabal. David sends his men to assist Nabal's servants with sheep-shearing. When David demands payment, Nabal refuses, incensing David. He pledges to take revenge by killing Nabal and confiscating his property. The servants alert Abigail to what is happening, and she acts quickly, gathering a large peace offering of bread, wine and other delicacies to take to him. She mounts a donkey and goes out to intercept David and his soldiers to try to save her household from destruction.

When she meets them on the road, she throws herself at David's feet and begs him to forgive her husband, adding that she didn't know about the request for payment. She goes on to predict David's destiny if he shows mercy: "When the Lord has fulfilled for my lord every good thing he promised concerning him, and has appointed him ruler over Israel, my lord will not have on his conscience the staggering burden of having avenged himself [on Nabal]." Her words are especially notable because she's the first person who prophesizes that David would one day become king. He accepts her apology and agrees not to kill her husband, who ends up dying 10 days later. David, no doubt recognizing Abigail's wisdom and good judgment, takes her as his wife. She is considered one of the seven Jewish women prophets.

Esther used only her words and wiles to save the Jews, making her an icon for oppressed people everywhere.

Protector of Her People

Her courageous action turns the tables on a dangerous enemy

he Book of Esther is somewhat controversial—some traditions do not recognize it as a canonical part of the Bible; others criticize it because the name of God is never mentioned in the text. But what a story! Esther, a Jewish girl in the non-Jewish land of Persia, grows into a beautiful and intelligent young woman under the tutelage of her uncle, Mordecai, who adopts her after the death of her parents. Persia's King Ahasuerus has stripped Queen Vashti of her royal title after she refused a summons to come to court, where he wished "to show the peoples and the officials her beauty." (Within the highly patriarchal Persian society, the men were afraid that Vashti's disobedience might lead to a spate of rebellious wives, and she was removed as queen in large part to reinforce the dominance of men within their households.)

The king's minions conduct a search throughout the land for a suitable replacement for the queen. Esther, "fair and beautiful"—and clearly very sharp— impresses the king, who "loved Esther more than all the other women" and names her his new queen. At Mordecai's suggestion, Esther has been keeping her Jewish heritage a secret, but when Haman, the king's top counselor, hatches a genocidal plot to murder the Jews throughout Persia, Esther acknowledges her heritage and saves the day. In a satisfying reversal, Haman and his sons are hung on the very gallows Haman constructed for Mordecai, and the would-be executioners throughout the land are killed by the Jewish communities they were sent to liquidate. And Esther—wise, strong Queen Esther—becomes the founder of the Jewish holiday of Purim, which celebrates the saving of her people. Esther remains the only woman to authorize a Jewish religious tradition.

According to legend, the column made of salt and rocks standing on the southern shore of the Dead Sea is a statue of Lot's wife.

The Nameless

In addition to the well-known female figures of the Bible, there are a host of other women who are unnamed but nonetheless play significant roles in biblical stories

Lot's Wife

In the Old Testament, who can forget Lot's wife? Despite the divine directive to *not* look back at the destruction being wrought on the sinful city of Sodom, she does anyway and is instantly transformed into a pillar of salt.

⟶ ◈ ⟵

Potiphar's Wife

Potiphar's spouse is a member of the Egyptian household where Joseph has been sold as a slave. Angry when Joseph resists her efforts to seduce him, she accuses him of rape—an offense for which Joseph is thrown into prison, only to escape when he impresses the Pharaoh with his ability to accurately interpret the Pharaoh's dreams along with those of other prisoners.

⟶ ◈ ⟵

Rescuer of Moses

The Pharaoh's daughter finds baby Moses in a basket that's nestled in the rushes by the banks of the Nile. She takes him into her home and raises him as her own, proving her generosity even further by hiring Jochebed, Moses' biological mother, as his wet nurse. (The Bible does not tell us whether she knew that Jochebed was Moses' mother, but it seems quite likely that she did.)

AMBAM

By rescuing Moses, the Pharaoh's daughter played a key role in the Israelites' eventual escape from slavery.

The Queen of Sheba

Further on in the Bible, we read about the Queen of Sheba, who visits Solomon along with her "very great retinue and camels bearing spices and very much gold and precious stones." She's heard of his fame and came to test him with "hard questions." The questions are not identified, but the queen is impressed with Solomon's wisdom: "The report was true that I heard in my own land of your accomplishments and of your wisdom, but I did not believe the reports until I came and my own eyes had seen it. Not even half had been told me; your wisdom and prosperity far surpass the report that I had heard. Happy are your wives!" After exchanging lavish gifts, the queen returns to her country, presumably somewhere in what was once known as Arabia.

The Witch of Endor

Equally anonymous was the Witch of Endor, visited by corrupt King Saul, who fears for his life as he faces the mighty forces of the Philistines. God has ceased responding to his prayers due to his wicked attempt to kill David and other acts of disobedience. Saul begs the witch to summon the recently deceased prophet Samuel that Saul might seek his counsel. The witch succeeds, but the ghost of Samuel offers Saul no comfort, predicting that he will fall to the Philistines and that "tomorrow you and your sons shall be with me" in the land of the dead.

The Witch of Endor did not give Saul the help he wanted.

The New Testament, too, is filled with anonymous women who make memorable appearances. Several come into direct contact with Jesus and exhibit extraordinary faith.

The woman at the well became an instant believer.

85

Samaritan Woman at the Well

Samaritans were much despised by the Jewish community in Israel, but this Samaritan woman hears the words of Jesus and believes; she immediately becomes a follower.

—◆◆◆—

Woman Suffering From Hemorrhages

This is the woman who reaches out to simply touch the hem of Jesus' garment as he passes through the crowd and is healed. "Your faith has made you well," Jesus tells her.

—◆◆◆—

The Adulterous Woman

When the pharisees bring this woman to Jesus while he is teaching in the temple, he quickly forgives her after challenging the judgmental crowd: "Let anyone among you who is without sin be the first to throw a stone at her." He sends her on her way with the simple directive: "Neither do I condemn you. Go your way, and from now on, do not sin again."

The Repentant Woman

This unidentified sinful woman kneels at Jesus' feet, weeping. Her tears mingle with the ointment she has brought with her as she kisses his feet, drying them with her hair and applying her salve. The Pharisee in whose house Jesus is dining is aghast that Jesus would allow such a woman to touch him in this way, but Jesus rejoices in the repentance of a sinner, noting that "her sins, which were many, have been forgiven; hence she has shown great love. But the one to whom little is forgiven, loves little." He tells the woman, "Your faith has saved you. Go in peace."

—◆◆◆—

Pilate's Wife

Finally, there is the wife of Pontius Pilate, the Roman governor given the task of deciding Jesus' fate. During Jesus' trial, she sends a message to her husband: "Have nothing to do with that innocent man, for today I have suffered a great deal because of a dream about him." Pilate ignores his wife's concerns and sentences Jesus to death, setting in motion the climactic chapter of the gospels.

Jesus offers forgiveness to both the adulterous woman (this page) and the repentant woman (opposite page, left), who falls at his feet in shame.

When Elizabeth (far left) and Mary met, each acknowledged the significance of the children they were carrying.

CHAPTER II

The New Testament

From Mary at his birth to Mary Magdalene
at his empty tomb, all of these women bore
witness to the divinity of Jesus

Christians' special devotion to Mary is partly due to her ordinariness—she's a loving parent and a devoted spouse, roles that are very relatable.

Mary

Mother of Jesus

She remains an iconic figure for Christians all over the world

"*And she gave birth to her firstborn, a son. She wrapped him in cloths and placed him in a manger, because there was no guest room available for them.*"

LUKE 2:7

Mary's role as the mother of Jesus has been one of the most common themes in Western art for many centuries.

Experts believe Mary was only around 16 when Jesus was born, which makes her courage all the more extraordinary.

Sweet, tender, faithful Mary, the mother of Jesus. No woman in history is more adored and venerated by Christians than she is. For centuries, her face and figure have adorned the sanctuaries of Christian churches, to be gazed at, admired, and in many places, even worshipped. Millions of believers, when faced with troubled times, continue to turn to her to intercede on their behalf. Her central role in the fundamental story of Christianity cannot be overstated.

Mary's place in Christian worship, particularly in the Catholic and Orthodox traditions, has certainly grown through the years, but the qualities we most associate with her are well supported by the biblical narrative. She first appears as an innocent young woman in the Galilean town of Nazareth, where the angel Gabriel appears to her. "Greetings, favored one!" he says. "The Lord is with you." The Bible describes Mary as being "perplexed," but surely this small-town girl, probably still in her

Michelangelo's drawings of the Madonna and child evinced the same tenderness as his sculpture *"Pietà"* (see page 99).

teens, felt more than a bit fearful as well. Gabriel reassures her: "Do not be afraid, Mary, for you have found favor with God. And, now, you will conceive in your womb and bear a son, and you will name him Jesus. He will be great, and will be called the Son of the Most High, and the Lord God will give to him the throne of his ancestor David. He will reign over the house of Jacob forever, and of his kingdom there will be no end."

The prediction of her son's future greatness might have been overwhelming enough for Mary, but she is also troubled by the very beginning of the angel's proclamation. Just how is she going to conceive and bear a son if she is still a virgin? This leads to another shocking proclamation from Gabriel: "The Holy Spirit will come upon you, and the power of the Most High will overshadow you; therefore the child to be born will be holy; he will be called Son of God."

Mary's response to perhaps the most amazing series of declarations in human history is one of the Bible's most stirring declarations of faith. "Here am I," she says, "the servant of the Lord; let it be with me according to your word." No skepticism, no objections, no worry about the likely shame to come her way as an unmarried, pregnant young woman—just acceptance of, and openness to, the will of God. In the Gospel of Matthew, we learn that Joseph received an angelic visit, too, assuring him that the child in Mary's womb was "from the Holy Spirit" and would "save his people from their sins." Rather than sending Mary away quietly, as he had planned when he first learned of her pregnancy, Joseph embraces Mary and takes her as his wife.

Soon we read the familiar but still wondrous tale of Christmas. Joseph and Mary travel to Bethlehem to be counted as part of the Roman census. All the local lodgings are full, so Mary and Joseph are forced to take shelter in a stable. There Mary gives birth to Jesus and lays him in a lowly manger, a rough-hewn container normally used to feed livestock. Luke tells us of the shepherds "keeping watch over their flock by night" and of a terrifying angelic appearance to them, of their visit to the babe, and of their report to Mary of the visitation and the glad tidings told them by the angel. Finally, we are told of the new mother's

Birthplace of Mary

The Church of St. Anne in the Old City of Jerusalem marks the site where many believe Joachim and Anne, the Virgin Mary's parents, lived—and where she was born. A previous church, built around 450 A.D. on this spot, was also dedicated to the Mother of God. With its austere stone exterior, the current church, which dates back to the 12th century, is a good example of medieval architecture. It is known for its remarkable acoustics, particularly well-suited for Gregorian chants.

"Greetings, favored one!" were the first words spoken during the angel's initial appearance (left) to Mary, in an event known throughout Christendom as the Annunciation. After Jesus was born, he was placed in a crude wooden manger (above).

"And Mary said, 'My soul magnifies the Lord, and my spirit rejoices in God my Savior, for he has looked with favor on the lowliness of his servant.'"

LUKE 1:46–47

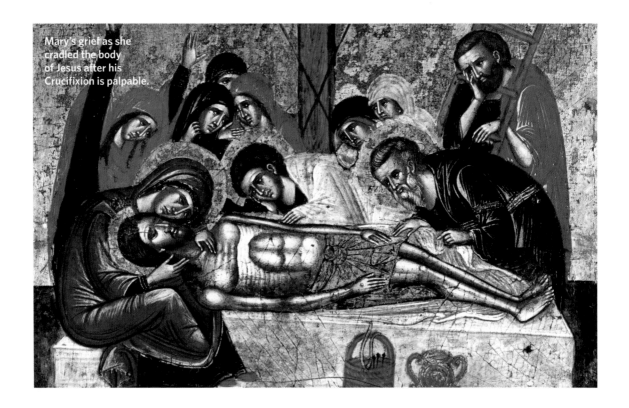

Mary's grief as she cradled the body of Jesus after his Crucifixion is palpable.

sweet response to all the hoopla: "But Mary treasured all these words and pondered them in her heart"—thoughtful, faithful Mary.

Matthew tells us of the three wise men sent by Herod to find the child "born king of the Jews" and of their use of a star whose brilliant light guides them to Jesus, and of the gifts they bring, and of their decision to avoid returning to Herod to protect the child from harm.

Mary appears several other times in the New Testament, always as a witness to Jesus's evolving mission. She is there when Jesus gets lost in bustling Jerusalem as a boy and his parents find him in the temple, discussing the meaning of scripture with far more senior teachers of the faith. "All who heard him were amazed at his understanding," the Bible tells us. Later, according to the Gospel of John, Mary is present at the agonizing moment when her son is crucified: "Meanwhile, standing near the cross of Jesus were his mother and his mother's sister, Mary the wife of Clopas, and Mary Magdalene. When Jesus saw his mother and the disciple whom he loved [commonly believed to be John] standing beside her, he said to his mother, 'Woman, here is your son.' Then he said to the disciple, 'Here is your mother.' And from that hour the disciple took her into his own home."

There is one final, brief reference to Mary in the Acts of the Apostles, where she is described as one of the founders of the early Christian church. And so, almost unique among women in the Bible, we see Mary from her youth, through her motherhood, and on to her full maturity as one of the senior leaders of the emerging Christian community.

> *"Meanwhile, standing near the cross of Jesus were his mother and his mother's sister, Mary the wife of Clopas, and Mary Magdalene."*
>
> *JOHN 19:25*

The most famous version of the *Pietà*—which means "pity" in English—is Michelangelo's, now housed in St. Peter's Basilica in Rome.

Mary is known by many titles; among the most popular are the Madonna, the Virgin Mary, the Mother of God, Our Lady, the Queen of Heaven and the Blessed Mother.

Mary's Tomb

The Church of the Sepulchre of Saint Mary in Jerusalem is built on the site of what many Christians believe is Mary's burial place. Upon entering the Crusader-era church, built into the side of a cave by Franciscan friars in the 14th century, there is a descending staircase dating from the 12th century. A chapel on one side honors Mary's parents; the other side features a chapel of St. Joseph. Downstairs, the chapel of Mary's tomb is a beautiful sanctuary bursting with iconography and medieval art.

Mary Magdalene

Steadfast Believer

The most loyal supporter of Jesus followed him even to the tomb

Because of her close
relationship with Jesus
and his followers,
Mary Magdalene is
sometimes called "the
apostle to the apostles."

According to John, Mary Magdalene was the first person to witness the empty tomb and encounter the risen Christ.

The popular conception of Mary Magdalene as a reformed prostitute has no biblical basis, nor does the idea that she was the bride at the wedding in Cana where Jesus turned water into wine, or any number of odd ideas that have surrounded this seminal figure in the history of Christianity. And while the Bible does record affection between her and Jesus, and perhaps even a kiss, those who conflate this evidence into a full-scale sexual relationship between the two are guilty of a massive overreach, at least in terms of the picture presented in the Gospels. What she *was*, as very clearly shown in the Gospel accounts, was Jesus' most loyal follower, who remained with him right to the end, even after many of his male disciples had deserted him.

She is first presented as one among a surprisingly large group of women who had been

The Gospels do not describe her as such but many Christians—and artists—have come to identify the woman who washes Jesus' feet as Mary Magdalene.

> *"The twelve were with him,
> as well as some women who had been
> cured of evil spirits and infirmities:
> Mary, called Magdalene, from whom
> seven demons had gone out...."*
>
> *LUKE 8:1–2*

"cured of evil spirits and infirmities" and were traveling with Jesus and his disciples, providing for them "out of their resources." The Bible tells us that the group included "Mary, called Magdalene, from whom seven demons had gone out." The number of demons suggests that Mary suffered from a serious illness; it does not in any sense suggest sexual promiscuity. The prominence of these women and their traveling together with men—extremely unusual for the time—in their support of Jesus' ministry was just one indication of how highly Jesus viewed women. A host of other anecdotes attest to his bestowing equal, and sometimes superior, status on women as opposed to their frequently feckless male counterparts.

Later, when Jesus is taken to the cross, Mary Magdalene is there again, watching and no doubt weeping as her Lord and Savior is nailed to the cross. Finally, it is Mary Magdalene, along with two other women, or alone—the details are a little different in each Gospel—who goes to Jesus' tomb to anoint his body with ointments and spices.

As they walk, the women are wondering how they will be able to reach the body, since they had

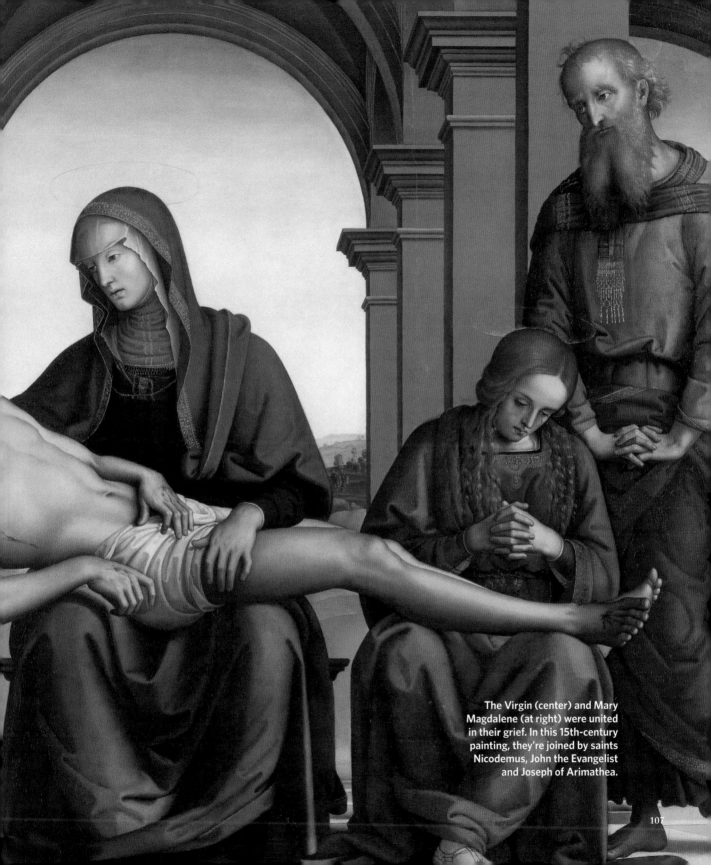

The Virgin (center) and Mary Magdalene (at right) were united in their grief. In this 15th-century painting, they're joined by saints Nicodemus, John the Evangelist and Joseph of Arimathea.

Though the false portrayal of Mary Magdalene as a prostitute was officially rejected by Pope Paul VI in 1969, the myth prevails in popular culture.

> *"Early on the first day of the week, while it was still dark, Mary Magdalene came to the tomb and saw that the stone had been removed from the tomb."*
>
> *JOHN 20:1*

seen an enormous stone rolled in front of it to block the entrance. But the stone has been rolled away and the tomb is empty. In John's account, Mary Magdalene visits the tomb alone and runs back to bring Peter and "the disciple Jesus loved"—often identified as John —to witness this miraculous event. Peter and John follow her to the tomb, confirm her findings and run back to tell the rest of the disciples. Mary remains behind, weeping. When she looks into the tomb, she sees "two angels in white, sitting where the body of Jesus had been lying." She asks them where the body of Jesus has been taken. Before she receives an answer, she turns around and suddenly sees a man standing there. At first she mistakes him for the gardener, and asks him, too, whether he knows the location of Jesus' body. "Mary!" he says to her. And in that moment she recognizes him as Jesus and cries out in Hebrew, "Rabbouni!" or "teacher." And so it came to pass that Mary Magdalene, faithful and strong, became the first person to see the risen Lord and the first to report his resurrection to the world.

"And now, your relative Elizabeth in her old age has also conceived a son; and this is the sixth month for her who was said to be barren. For nothing will be impossible with God."

LUKE 1:36–37

The meeting between Mary (in blue) and Elizabeth was an occasion of great joy for both women.

Elizabeth

The Forerunner

Mary's cousin is the first to recognize the divinity of Jesus

Elizabeth and her husband, Zechariah, are described in the Bible as "righteous before God, living blamelessly according to all the commandments and regulations of the Lord." Zechariah was a priest and Elizabeth was descended from a priestly family. But the couple shared a great sadness: Elizabeth had been unable to conceive and was now too old to hope for a child. Then, in one of the New Testament's many examples of God using unlikely vessels to touch human history, Elizabeth and Zechariah, old though they may be, become key players in the events that lead to the birth of Jesus.

First the angel Gabriel appears to a terrified Zechariah and tells him that his prayers have been answered and that Elizabeth will become pregnant at last and give birth to a son: "You will have joy and gladness, and many will rejoice at his birth, for he will be great in the sight of the Lord." Zechariah's understandable skepticism is punished by Gabriel, who strikes him unable to speak until the birth of Zechariah's son, John, who grows up to become the great forerunner of Jesus known as John the Baptist.

The second act belongs to the women: first to Elizabeth's cousin Mary, who has also been visited by an angel and informed that she too will conceive and bear a son who "will be great and will be called the Son of the Most High," and then to Elizabeth, who becomes the first person in the Bible to recognize the divinity of Jesus when the child in her womb leaps for joy when a pregnant Mary arrives for a visit. "Blessed are you among women," Elizabeth cries, "and blessed is the fruit of your womb. And why has this happened to me, that the mother of my Lord comes to me?"

The focus returns to Zechariah in the final act, when he miraculously regains his speech after the birth of his son and declares the coming of the Savior and the role of his son, John, as the one "who will go before the Lord to prepare his ways."

Zechariah and Elizabeth disappear from the biblical narrative after these events, but Elizabeth is still revered as a saint in the Catholic, Orthodox and Anglican traditions.

Martha

Sister of Lazarus

After chiding a tardy Jesus, she witnesses his greatest miracle

Martha makes two appearances in the Gospel narratives. In the first, in the Gospel of Luke, she is a harried hostess, scrambling around her home, perhaps preparing food and cleaning up, while her sister Mary sits at the feet of Jesus, listening to what he is saying. "Lord," Martha cries in frustration, "do you not care that my sister has left me to do all the work by myself? Tell her then to help me." Many of us probably sympathize with Martha's complaint, but Jesus, as he often did, makes a surprising response: "Martha, Martha, you are worried and distracted by many things; there is need of only one thing. Mary has chosen the better part, which will not be taken away from her." Set aside the distracting details of life, Jesus seems to be saying, all the day-to-day worries that preoccupy us, and focus on the things that really matter. Luke places this story between the tale of the Good Samaritan, which illustrates the nature of genuine compassion, and Jesus's recitation of the Lord's Prayer, which remains a fundamental component of almost every form of Christian worship. Together the three present the defining elements of a spiritual life: ethical action (Good Samaritan), contemplation and learning (Mary and Martha), and prayer (the Lord's Prayer).

Martha appears again in the Gospel of John, as the sister of Lazarus—a man beloved of Jesus—who is sick and near death. Jesus, not believing the illness to be serious, delays visiting Lazarus and by the time he arrives in Bethany, Lazarus has been "in the tomb four days." What follows is Jesus's final and greatest miracle, the one that John presents as precipitating his arrest and crucifixion. Martha, hearing that Jesus is coming, runs out to meet him. At first, she reproaches him: "Lord, if you had been here, my brother would not have died." Jesus responds: "Your brother will rise again." But Martha misunderstands, thinking Jesus is referring to the general resurrection on the last day. Jesus tells her: "I am the resurrection and the life. Those who believe in me, even though they die, will live." When Jesus sees Mary and the crowd with her weeping inconsolably, he is moved and begins to weep, too. He walks to the tomb and demands that the stone be rolled away from its opening. But Martha objects: "Lord, already there is a stench because he has been dead four days." Jesus insists, and after the stone is rolled away, he cries out with a loud voice, "Lazarus, come out!" Then, in Luke's vivid description, "The dead man came out, his hands and feet bound with strips of cloth, and his face wrapped in a cloth. Jesus said to them, 'Unbind him, and let him go.'"

"Martha said to Jesus, 'Lord,
if you had been here, my brother
would not have died. But even now
I know that God will give you
whatever you ask of him.'"

JOHN 11:21–22

Despite the stench of death
surrounding the tomb, Jesus (with
Mary at his feet and Martha beside him)
raised Lazarus from the dead.

113

"*But when Herod's birthday came, the daughter of Herodias danced before the company, and she pleased Herod so much that he promised on oath to grant her whatever she might ask.*"

JOHN 14:6–7

As this painting suggests, perhaps Salome was not as interested in the head of John as her mother was. The Bible does not tell us.

Salome

Deathly Dancer

Her performance led to the martyrdom of one of Christianity's first prophets

Salome and her mother, Herodias, belong with Delilah and Jezebel among the ranks of the Bible's most notorious female villains. Herodias and King Herod Antipas (the grandson of the Herod who had ordered the murder of Jewish children at the time of Jesus' birth) had committed an abomination in the eyes of John the Baptist by leaving their spouses and marrying each other, despite the fact that Herodias' previous husband was Herod's brother, Philip. "It is not lawful for you to have your brother's wife," John declared, instantly incurring the wrath of Herodias. At her request, Herod has John arrested, though allegedly he was afraid of John, "knowing that he was a righteous and holy man." On his birthday, Herod, a far more passive version of his famously brutal grandfather, throws a lavish banquet "for his courtiers and officers and for the leaders of Galilee." Herodias' daughter, Salome, perhaps 16 years old, performs a dance that so pleases Herod and his guests that he offers to give her whatever she wants, "even half of my kingdom." Salome rushes to her mother to ask her how she

According to Mark 6:21, "On his birthday, Herod gave a banquet for his high officials and military commanders and the leading men of Galilee."

should respond to this extravagant offer. Herodias tells her daughter what to ask for and Salome immediately passes the request along to Herod: "I want you to give me at once the head of John the Baptist on a platter." Having made his pledge in front of all his guests, Herod is forced to comply. John is summarily executed and his head is brought into the banquet on a platter and given to Salome, who immediately passes it to her mother. Some have speculated that this series of events was orchestrated in advance by Herodias and Herod—would he really have given Salome half his kingdom?—as a means to murder John without Herod having to take the blame, though as king, in spite of his promise, he could have rejected Salome's request. The Bible concludes the story by telling us that Jesus' disciples "came and took [John's] body, and laid it in a tomb." What became of John's head, we do not know.

Artists usually
portray Salome
as a dangerous
seductress.

Tabitha, also known as Dorcas, was so beloved, mourners beseeched Peter to raise her from the dead.

"Peter…knelt down and prayed. He turned to the body and said, 'Tabitha, get up.' Then she opened her eyes, and seeing Peter, she sat up. He gave her his hand and helped her up. Then calling the saints and widows, he showed her to be alive. This became known throughout Joppa, and many believed in the Lord."

ACTS 9:40-42

Tabitha

Altruist Resurrected

A believer renowned for her generosity was brought back to life by Peter's prayers

Although the resurrections of Jesus Christ and Lazarus are the best known in the Bible, Tabitha, an early devotee of the church, was also raised from the dead through a heavenly miracle that helped spread belief in the Messiah. A beloved fixture in the city of Joppa, a port near modern-day Tel Aviv in Israel, Tabitha—also known as Dorcas—is portrayed as a disciple who was "full of good works and acts of charity." She is believed to have been independently wealthy and a talented seamstress, who gave liberally to the poor and sewed garments for the needy, especially widows. She may have even been a widow herself, as there is no mention of family in her home.

In both Luke and Acts, we're told that Tabitha becomes ill and dies, prompting a wide outpouring of grief among the community where she had played such an essential role. Mourners laid out her body in an upper room of her home to prepare it for burial. But unable to accept her death, they eventually call for the apostle Peter to come. When he arrives, Peter prays over Tabitha's corpse on bended knee, asking God to intervene. Lo and behold, Tabitha rises from the dead.

As word of the miracle spreads throughout Joppa, scores of new believers are drawn to the church. In life, Tabitha's good works made her a prime example of a kindly woman who took seriously Jesus' admonishment to care for the needy. And through her resurrection, Tabitha became a symbol of God's mercy and a message of hope to the faithful and true.

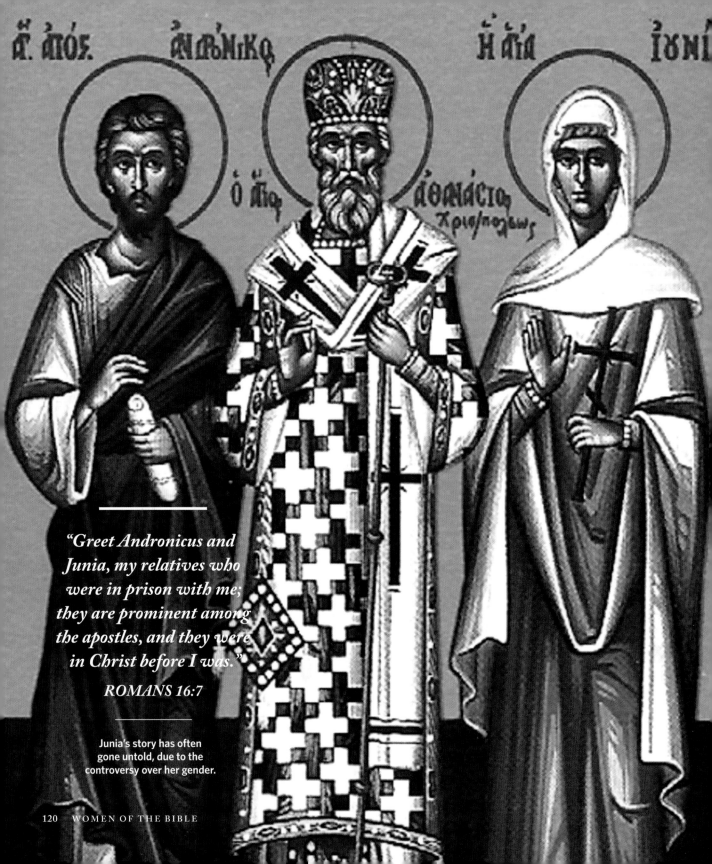

 Α. ΑΠΟ. ΑΝΔΡΟΝΙΚΟ Η ΑΓΙΑ ΙΥΝΙ
Ο ΑΓΙΟ ΑΘΑΝΑΣΙΟ Χρισ/πολεως

> "*Greet Andronicus and Junia, my relatives who were in prison with me; they are prominent among the apostles, and they were in Christ before I was.*"
>
> **ROMANS 16:7**

Junia's story has often gone untold, due to the controversy over her gender.

Junia
Mystery Apostle

A valuable leader in the early church of Rome, she has stirred debate for centuries

There's a long-running argument over whether Junia, an apostle in the early church, was actually a woman or a man. But the gender confusion is likely due to a change in the spelling of her name years later by Bible translators who were uncomfortable with the idea of a woman being an "apostle," so her name was altered to the masculine Junias. Before the 13th century, Junia was unanimously referred to as a woman—even by the Archbishop of Constantinople John Chrysostom, who was not considered an advocate of women. In the fourth century, he wrote of Junia, "O how great is the devotion of this woman that she should be counted worthy of the appellation of apostle!"

St. Paul also had high praise for Junia, whom he identified as his "kinsman and fellow prisoner." It was common for the early Christians in pagan Rome to be persecuted and imprisoned for their beliefs—and Junia was outspoken enough to be incarcerated for a time, perhaps in the cramped, miserable Mamertine prison, the remains of which still stand overlooking the Roman Forum. According to Romans 16:7, Junia had become a Christian before Paul, and since his conversion occurred just a few years after the resurrection of Christ, this would make her one of the earliest members of the church in Rome. She may have even traveled to Jerusalem for Passover and seen the Crucifixion or, later, the ascension of the resurrected Jesus. In any case, her fervor and steadfastness were so profound that Paul deemed her "prominent among the apostles," and she was still ministering in the church when Paul sent his Letter to the Romans in A.D. 57. Her remarkable story—and the suppression of it—stands as a reminder of the many visionary women whose names have been forgotten, but whose impact rightly deserves celebration.

"A certain woman named Lydia, a worshipper of God, was listening to us; she was from the city of Thyatira and a dealer in purple cloth. The Lord opened her heart to listen eagerly to what was said by Paul. When she and her household were baptized, she urged us, saying, 'If you have judged me to be faithful to the Lord, come and stay at my home.'"

ACTS 16:14-15

Lydia, commonly identified as a merchant of purple cloth, is known as the "patroness of dyers."

Lydia

First European Convert

A successful businesswoman, she is pivotal in spreading the teachings of Jesus

During St. Paul's second missionary journey, he had a vision that brought him to Macedonia, a region north of modern-day Greece. Upon arrival, he and his team headed for the city of Philippi, a Roman colony, where they ministered—first, not to men, but to a group of women who had gathered for prayer. That group included Lydia, originally from the city of Thyatira, where she had built a business as a prominent dealer in expensive purple cloth, an artisanal commodity for which the city was known. Although she was religious, Lydia was a Jew and not a believer in Christ. She received Paul's ministry with an "open heart" and thus earned the distinction of becoming his first documented convert to Christianity on the European continent.

Lydia embraced her new faith with much the same ardor that fueled her business success as a luxury fabric merchant. She and her family were baptized in the river Zygaktis, and she immediately opened her villa to Paul and his companions, Silas and Timothy. Her home became a center for a growing number of converts in Philippi who gathered for prayer and worship. Paul's sojourn in Philippi was interrupted when he and Silas were arrested and imprisoned by Roman magistrates for the crime of "casting out demons." We are told that God set them free in the night with an earthquake that broke their shackles, and the two men went straight back to the house of Lydia to regroup.

Although Paul and his companions quickly moved on, continuing their journey through the ancient world, Lydia's hospitality is credited with providing a base for the first Christian church in Macedonia—making her a central figure in the growing religious movement.

"There he found a Jew named Aquila, a native of Pontus, who had recently come from Italy with his wife Priscilla, because Claudius had ordered all Jews to leave Rome. Paul went to see them, and, because he was of the same trade, he stayed with them."

ACTS 18:2–3

Priscilla and her husband, Aquila, greatly assisted Paul (seated) in the establishment of the early Christian church among the Gentiles.

Priscilla

Church Builder

Widely traveled, she plays a major role in the early church

Priscilla is one of the founders of the Christian church and a close friend of Paul's, who spreads the word of the Gospel throughout the ancient world. She, along with her husband, Aquila—seemingly the less active of the pair—first meet Paul in Corinth, where they have traveled after being expelled from Rome by an edict of the Emperor Claudius that banned all people of Jewish faith from living in the city. Paul stays with the couple for some time, practicing their common trade of tentmaking (some suggest this may more generally refer to work with leather) and presumably sharing his understanding of the faith. Later, Priscilla moves to Ephesus, where her home

becomes a thriving early church and she instructs a scholar named Apollos, who goes on to spread the Gospel further. She next appears in Paul's Letter to the Romans, in which he directs his readers to "greet Prisca [Priscilla's formal name] and Aquila, who work with me in Christ Jesus, and who risked their necks for my life, to whom not only I give thanks, but also all the churches of the Gentiles." The final reference to her is in Paul's second letter to Timothy, his faithful disciple, to whom he entrusts the future of the church he has done so much to build. As he sits in a Roman jail cell awaiting his execution, he sends greetings to a very small group of fellow Christians; at the top of the list are Priscilla and Aquila.

"I commend to you our sister Phoebe, a deacon of the church at Cenchreae, so that you may welcome her in the Lord as is fitting for the saints, and help her in whatever she may require from you, for she has been a benefactor of many and of myself as well."

ROMANS 16:1-2

A Greek convert, Phoebe safely transported Paul's manuscript, which would become the basis for Christian theology.

Phoebe

Trusted Messenger

A pillar of the early Christian church, she becomes Paul's emissary to Rome

hurch historians have long believed that Phoebe was the person whom the apostle Paul entrusted to travel to Rome with his letter to the believers there—the epistle that would become the Book of Romans in the New Testament. Phoebe is portrayed as a strong and influential member of the early Christian movement, and her designation as "deacon" indicates that she held an important position within the church at Cenchreae, a seaport some eight miles from Corinth in Greece, where Paul was staying at the time. Paul refers to Phoebe as a benefactor of many—himself included—giving the impression that she is a woman of means who freely donates her money to support those in need and to bolster his missionary endeavors.

Interestingly, in the early days of the burgeoning Christian church, women often held equal status with men and were treated without prejudice. Phoebe was clearly one such woman, an upstanding and authoritative member of the community who helps build the foundation of the congregation.

Even more impressive is Phoebe's willingness as a woman to undertake the arduous journey from Greece to Rome in the first century A.D. with Paul's letter. The apostle clearly has the highest regard for her intelligence and reliability when he designates her to be his messenger. And Phoebe proves her worth, establishing herself as a key figure in history by delivering what would turn out to be one of the most famous and influential letters of all time.

The Saints

While the women in
the Bible were the
first foundational
females of faith, women have
figured prominently in a host
of religious communities in
the many centuries since
the book's composition.
The Catholic tradition, in
particular, has honored
hundreds of women as saints
and patron saints, many of
whom continue to attract the
prayers of the faithful
to this day. Here
are several of the most
prominent and beloved.

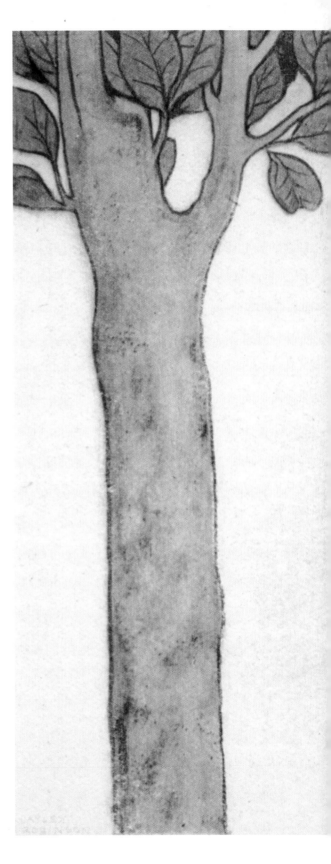

Although she doesn't
get a parade like
St. Patrick, St. Brigid
is one of Ireland's
patron saints.

The 24th of 25 children, St. Catherine of Siena was born during the height of the Black Death.

St. Catherine of Siena (1347-1380)

Only 5 when she experienced her first vision of Christ, Catherine vowed at that moment to devote her life to God. Refusing to marry, she became a lay Dominican, traveling widely to promote repentance and negotiate truces between Florence and Rome (then independent cities) and various feuding church factions. Her spiritual writings were hugely influential, and she was named a Doctor of the Church because of her contributions to theology. She's also the patron saint of Italy (along with St. Francis of Assisi) and of Europe.

The Teresas

There are many saints named Teresa; the best known are St. Teresa of Ávila (1515-1582), the Spanish mystic whose writings continue to attract attention from theologians and laypeople alike; St. Thérèse of Lisieux (1873-1897), "The Little Flower," a Carmelite nun who is associated with the Little Way, a spiritual practice that converts even the smallest actions into a form of prayer; and most recently, St. Teresa of Calcutta (1910-1997), known to the world as Mother Teresa, whose work among the poor in India earned her the admiration of millions.

St. Teresa of Calcutta, aka Mother Teresa, has come to represent the very essence of charity.

Joan of Arc (1412–1431)

She is perhaps the most famous female saint. Also known as the Maid of Orleans, she led the French to victory in battle at the age of 18. She later resisted all efforts to persuade her to renounce her faith and was burned at the stake as a heretic.

———◆———

St. Bernadette
(1844–1879)

A favorite of many contemporary Catholics, St. Bernadette (pictured) was a poor, uneducated girl who received a startling series of visions of Mary in the grotto of Massabielle near Lourdes, France, now a pilgrimage site for Christians who travel from far away to visit the shrine to her visions and bathe in the healing waters there.

"God is always present. Nothing happens without His permission or outside of His will. Anything we do to others we do to Him. All kindness and goodness are in Him."
St. Bernadette

The tale of Joan of Arc has been told and retold through the ages since her death.

Mrs Wm Seaton. 1797.

St. Elizabeth Ann Seton (1744-1821)

She was the first native-born American to be canonized by the Roman Catholic Church. She put her faith into action by establishing schools and founding the religious order the Sisters of Charity in 1809. For centuries, the order has assisted orphans, the poor and other destitute people in a variety of communities around the country. A shrine devoted to her is located at the very tip of Manhattan.

Saint Brigid of Ireland (circa 453-524)

Born a slave, she founded two monasteries and is best remembered for her generosity, giving away all she had to the poor, including, famously, her father's treasured sword to a beggar who was struggling to feed his family. Legend says she prayed to God to be made ugly, so no man would desire her, a prayer that was answered until she took her final vows as a nun and her beauty was restored.

Numerous places in Ireland are named Kilbride, after St. Brigid ("Kilbride" means "church of Brigid").

135

An author (St. Faustina, top), a long-suffering mother (St. Monica, (bottom), and a sickly young woman (St. Kateri Tekakwitha, opposite page) have all been canonized.

St. Faustina (1905-1938)

Known as the Apostle of Divine Mercy, she wrote a diary about her visions of Jesus and his communications with her that still inspires Christians today.

* ✦ *

St. Monica (circa 322-387)

Best remembered as the mother of the influential theologian St. Augustine, she prayed for his soul for 17 years as he plunged into a dissolute existence devoted to the pleasures of the flesh before converting later in life.

* ✦ *

St. Kateri Tekakwitha (1656-1680)

Known as Lily of the Mohawks, she was the first Native American saint. A convert to Christianity at 19, St. Kateri took a vow of chastity and pledged herself to Jesus alone. Her face, which had been scarred by smallpox, was miraculously cleansed of all marks when she died at the age of 24.

The Church of the
Holy Sepulchre in
Jerusalem is one
of the holiest sites
in Christianity.

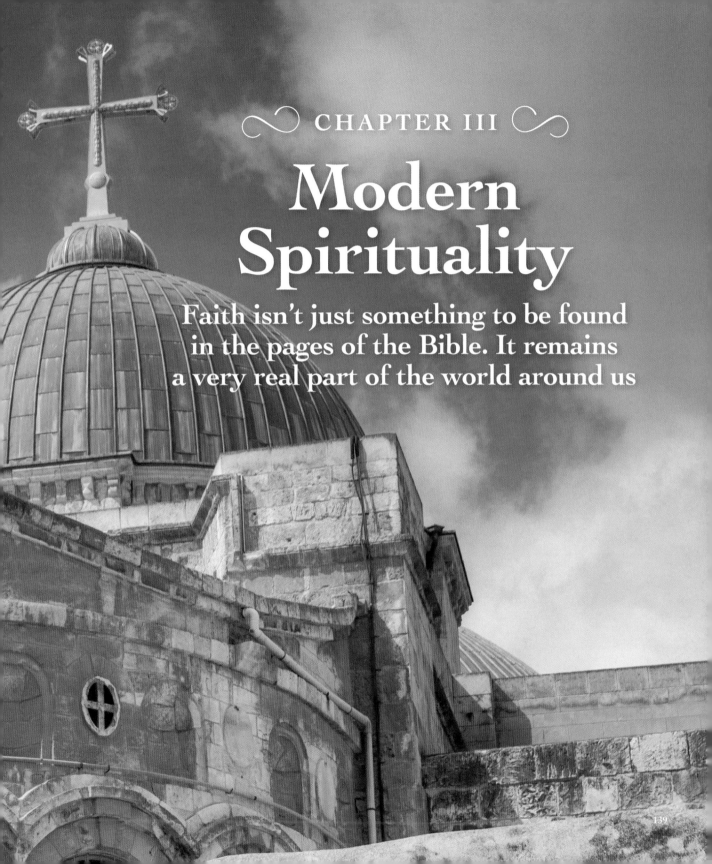

CHAPTER III

Modern Spirituality

Faith isn't just something to be found in the pages of the Bible. It remains a very real part of the world around us

Our Lady of Lourdes
Shrine, France

𝕸ary's 𝕾hrines

Roman Catholics worldwide reveal their love for the Blessed Virgin with statues, shrines and endless celebrations

C atholics love to pay homage to the Virgin Mary, and they like to do so with very public displays of devotion. Even in recent years, oversize statues of the Blessed Mother are still being erected around the globe, and pilgrimages to Marian shrines continue at a brisk pace. (A Marian shrine marks a spot where a Marian apparition—a documented supernatural appearance by the Virgin Mary—occurred; it can also be a place where Our Lady is believed to have performed a miracle. Approval by the local bishop or the Vatican is also necessary.) Although historically, Europe is where most apparitions have been reported, the U.S. has many of its own; there are hundreds of Marian shrines located across all 50 states.

Our Lady of Lourdes Shrine, France

In 1858, a 14-year-old girl experienced 18 apparitions of a lady in a white veil; the church recognized the authenticity of the events in 1862. Today, almost 6 million pilgrims visit the world-famous shrine in Lourdes annually, many of them seeking cures in the healing waters of the "miraculous spring."

✦❖✦

The Shrine of Our Lady of La Leche, Florida

The first Marian shrine in the U.S.—the site in St. Augustine traces its history back to 1565, when Spanish sailors arrived in the New World to convert Native Americans to Christianity—remains a popular pilgrimage site. Here, devotees seek intercession for conception and successful pregnancies. The centerpiece of the shrine is a statue of the Virgin nursing the infant Jesus. The original chapel was destroyed in 1728 during the British siege of St. Augustine; the next structure succumbed to a hurricane. The current cozy chapel (it seats 30) was built in 1914. Visitors can also enjoy a small museum that focuses on the religious motivations and methods of the Spanish explorers.

A noon mass is held each day for pilgrims visiting this Florida shrine.

The Virgen de la Paz, in Venezuela in the Andes, is the tallest Marian statue in the world. It marks a spot where the Virgin reportedly appeared in 1570.

Virgen de la Paz, Venezuela

This 1,200-ton statue, made entirely of concrete, watches over the city of Trujillo from atop a nearby hill. When it opened in 1983, "the Monument of Peace" was the tallest statue in the Americas. (At 153 feet, it is taller than the Statue of Liberty, minus the base.) Visitors can climb a staircase and stop at five different observation points.

Virgen de la Paz, Venezuela

Virgen del Socavón, Bolivia

When this 149-foot statue, which means "Our Lady of the Mineshaft," was unveiled atop a mountain in the mining town of Oruro, in February 2013, it instantly became one of the largest Marian statues in the world. Thousands of people march in procession through Oruro's streets during the annual four-day carnival that precedes Lent. You can take a cable car to the top of the statue for incredible views of the surrounding countryside.

Sanctuary of Our Lady of Fátima, Portugal

With almost 5 million pilgrims making the trek here annually, this is one of the largest and most visited Marian shrines in the world. The backstory: Between May and October 1917, the Virgin Mary appeared once a month to three shepherd children in the fields just outside of the small town of Fátima. Her main message at the time (World War I was raging) was to pray for world peace.

Basilica of the National Shrine of the Immaculate Conception, Washington, D.C.

This shrine, the largest Catholic Church in North America and a lovely example of neo-Byzantine architecture, has 81 chapels honoring the Blessed Mother.

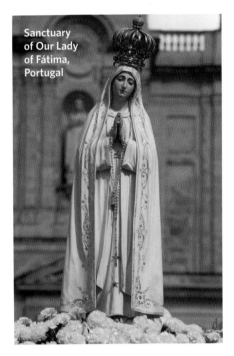

Sanctuary of Our Lady of Fátima, Portugal

Virgen del Socavón, Bolivia

Basilica of the National Shrine of the Immaculate Conception, Washington, D.C.

Our Lady of the
Sacred Heart,
France

Our Lady of the Sacred Heart, France

Completed at the end of World War II, this is the largest statue of the Virgin Mary in Europe, the tallest religious statue in France and a popular pilgrimage destination. You can climb about 150 steps in the statue to access the terrace (located in Mary's crown) and take in the stunning views around Mirabel-Ain, a small town in the southeast corner of the country.

Shrine of Our Lady of Guadalupe, Mexico

In 1531, the Virgin Mary appeared to Juan Diego, an older Aztec man, and told him to build a church at the site. To prove his claims, the Virgin imprinted an image of herself on a piece of his clothing. Almost 500 years later, this vast complex in Mexico City is considered the most-visited Marian shrine in the world. (The imprinted tilma is on display here.) Our Lady of Guadalupe is now the patron saint of both North and South America, but she remains particularly beloved in Mexico, where even the non-religious appreciate her symbolic power. Finally, in 2002, Diego was canonized a saint.

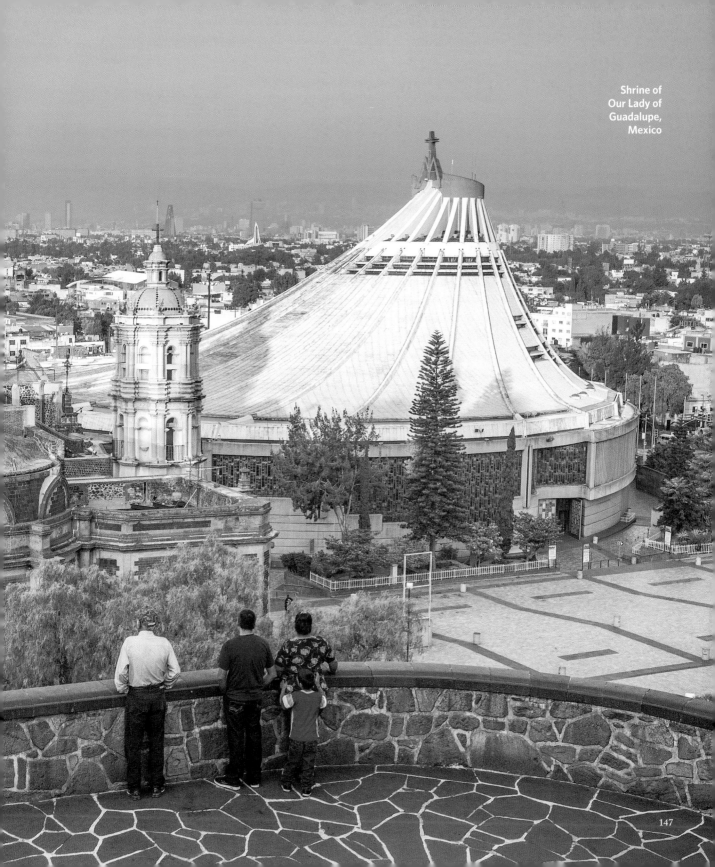

Shrine of
Our Lady of
Guadalupe,
Mexico

Black Madonna of
Częstochowa, Poland

Black Madonna of Częstochowa, Poland

The origins of the icon, which is housed in the most popular shrine in the country, are shrouded in mystery. While it's been in Poland for at least 600 years, one legend claims that St. Luke painted it on a cedar tabletop at the house of the Holy Family. Pope John Paul II said he secretly visited "the Queen and Protector of Poland" in Częstochowa during World War II.

Fervent Feasts

Marian feast days are holy days recognized by Catholics to celebrate pivotal events in the life of the Virgin Mary. While there are literally hundreds of feast days, the Roman Catholic Church recognizes three main ones, including the Birth of Mary on September 8 and the Feast of the Immaculate Conception on December 8. But perhaps the most widely celebrated of all is August 15's Feast of the Assumption, which celebrates the moment when Mary's body and soul were whisked up to heaven at the end of her earthly life. Many Catholic countries worldwide, including Italy, France, Spain and Poland, mark this as a national holiday. While not a public holiday in the U.S., many American Catholics do attend Mass and mark the day with fireworks and food. Cleveland, Ohio, is home to the largest Feast of the Assumption party in the country. The four-day festival has been held for more than 120 years and kicks off on August 12 in the city's Little Italy district.

Feast of the Assumption, Cleveland

Mother of Mercy

The image of Mary is ubiquitous both here in the United States and in nations around the globe, particularly those with thriving Catholic communities. In the pictures that follow, we present just a small sample of the various settings in which the Blessed Virgin has appeared. In an era when some question the future of Christianity, Mary is still very clearly going strong.

The Virgin of El Rocío, a small carved wooden statue in Almonte, Spain, attracts nearly a million visitors each year in an annual procession.

In Cuba, Christians and
followers of the Yoruba
religion both worship the
Virgin of Regla, sometimes
called the Black Madonna.

Mary is honored by many Mexicans as the Virgin of Guadalupe. Her appearance to a peasant named Juan Diego in 1531 is celebrated every year on December 12. These pilgrims celebrated the festivities in Mexico City in 2014.

The residents of Clifden, County Galway, Ireland, created this makeshift shrine to the Virgin Mary outside a bar as part of a Catholic parade through their village in 2010.

157

Catholics from Sri Lanka traveled to Rome in 2017 to participate in a parade in honor of the Virgin Mary and Mary's Month, traditionally recognized as May. The procession ended at the Church of the Twelve Holy Apostles.

A Tour of the Holy Land

It's one thing to read about key figures in the Bible and quite another to see where they lived, worked and raised their families. Follow their paths in these ancient, historic locales

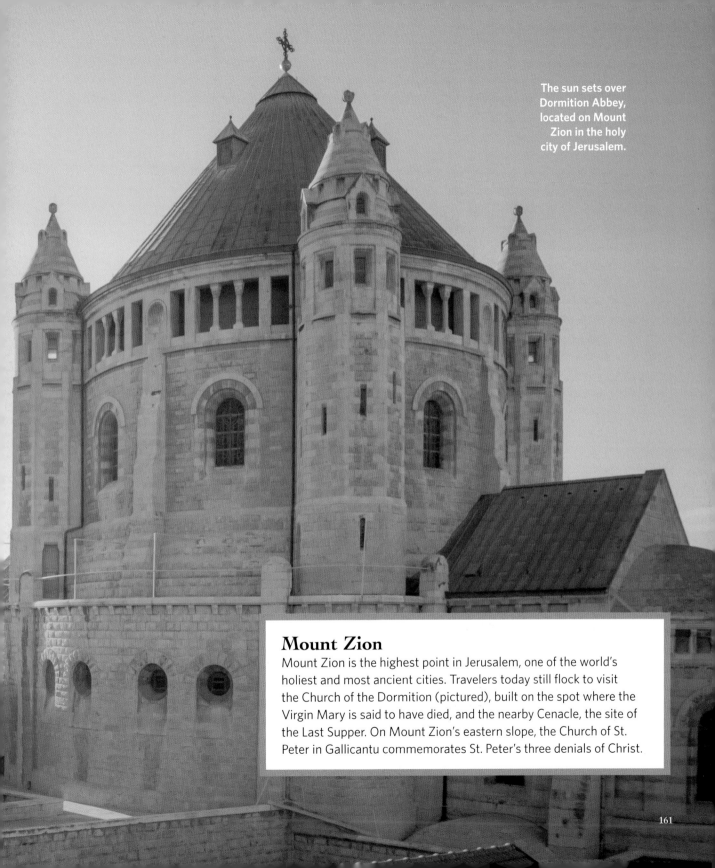

The sun sets over Dormition Abbey, located on Mount Zion in the holy city of Jerusalem.

Mount Zion

Mount Zion is the highest point in Jerusalem, one of the world's holiest and most ancient cities. Travelers today still flock to visit the Church of the Dormition (pictured), built on the spot where the Virgin Mary is said to have died, and the nearby Cenacle, the site of the Last Supper. On Mount Zion's eastern slope, the Church of St. Peter in Gallicantu commemorates St. Peter's three denials of Christ.

The Lutheran Church of the Redeemer's bell tower overlooks the Christian Quarter.

The Christian Quarter

One of four quarters that make up the Old City of Jerusalem (the other three are the Jewish Quarter, Muslim Quarter and Armenian quarters), the Christian Quarter is home to the Church of the Holy Sepulchre (see page 164), and the Via Dolorosa (the route of the Stations of the Cross—see page 166). Though religious buildings occupy most of the quarter, there are also many restaurants, stores and hotels (many of which were built by various churches). Many pilgrims consider a visit here the highlight of their trip to the Holy Land.

Mount of Olives

A series of limestone ridges, the Mount of Olives in Jerusalem has been a Jewish cemetery for over 3,000 years. Jesus would have passed by it as he made his triumphal entry into the city on Palm Sunday. Today, the stunning Russian Orthodox Church of Mary Magdalene (pictured) is one of several holy sites travelers can visit. Nearby, on the grounds of the Church of All Nations, is the Garden of Gethsemane, where Jesus prayed before his arrest.

Christians from around the world come to take part in observances at the Church of the Holy Sepulchre.

Church of the Holy Sepulchre

After his conversion to Christianity in 312, the Emperor Constantine ordered that a temple of Venus in Jerusalem be demolished and replaced with a church on this sacred place, the site of Jesus' crucifixion and of the tomb where he was buried. It was destroyed by fire and earthquake and rebuilt several times; the current building dates to the 12th century. A pilgrimage destination since the fourth century (the final five Stations of the Cross are located within its walls), today it is a sprawling complex comprised of over 30 Roman Catholic and Orthodox chapels. Visitors of all religions are welcome, however. Not surprisingly, it's often crowded, so insiders advise that you arrive early.

Stations of the Cross

Also known as the Via Dolorosa (the Way of Suffering), the 14 Stations of the Cross follow the path along which Jesus was forced to carry his cross from where he was condemned to death to the Crucifixion site on Golgotha, now the Church of the Holy Sepulchre. The route stretches about 2,000 feet; nine stations are outside the church, and the final five are inside it. Every Friday, Franciscans conduct a Way of the Cross tour that follows the traditional route—an especially moving devotion when following in Jesus' actual footsteps.

Portions of the Via Dolorosa have been excavated and can be followed through Jerusalem's Old City.

Bethlehem

Not only is it where Jesus was born, but it's also the place where King David was anointed king of Israel. The town's highlight is the Church of the Nativity—one of the oldest Christian churches—and the underground grotto in the church's crypt, said to be the spot where Jesus was born (expect long lines as it's an understandably popular attraction). Today, Bethlehem is a bustling city located 5 miles from Jerusalem; it's best to go by private transportation since Israeli public transit can't enter the West Bank.

The lantern in the Church of the Annunciation's cupola symbolizes the Light of the World.

Nazareth

An ancient city in northern Israel, Nazareth is most famous as Jesus' childhood home. Not surprisingly, it's a major pilgrimage destination, with numerous shrines, churches and monasteries the devout can visit. Perhaps the most popular is the Church of the Annunciation, the largest Christian shrine in the Middle East, which is said to be where the angel Gabriel announced to Mary that she would give birth to the son of God. The church has been destroyed and rebuilt numerous times; the present-day building dates to 1969.

Sea of Galilee

Located in Israel's northern region, this is the lowest freshwater lake on Earth. Much of Jesus' ministry took place along its shores, and a number of his apostles, including Simon, Andrew, John, James and Matthew, hailed from Galilean fishing villages. Jesus delivered the Sermon on the Mount on a hill overlooking the lake, and many of his miracles occurred here, including his walking on water, calming the storm and the miraculous catch of fish. Today, visitors can walk around the lake on the Sea of Galilee Trail, or hike the Jesus Trail from Nazareth to Capernaum on its northern shore.

St. George's Monastery
This otherworldly structure that appears to cling to the side of a steep cliff is located in the Wadi Qelt river canyon in the Judean Desert, about 5 miles from Jericho. It dates back to the fourth century and is comprised of the Church of the Holy Virgin and the Church of St. George and St. John, which boasts incredible Byzantine mosaics. The area is also believed to be the location of the valley of the shadow of death mentioned in Psalm 23, and where the parable of the Good Samaritan was set.

Capernaum

Now known as Kfar Nahum, this was a thriving fishing village in Jesus' time. Cited in all four Gospels, it was here that Jesus gave the "Bread of Life" sermon in the town's synagogue, the ruins of which can be visited, along with a structure thought to have been Peter's home. Jesus also performed several miracles here, including expelling a demon and healing Peter's mother-in-law.

Mount Tabor

Mount Tabor, 9 miles west of the Sea of Galilee, is thought to be where the Transfiguration of Jesus took place—what St. Thomas Aquinas called "the greatest miracle." After Jesus led Peter, James and John up the mountain to pray, he suddenly became "radiant in glory" and Elijah and Moses appeared alongside him. Then a voice said, "This is my Son, whom I love; with him I am well pleased. Listen to him!" Today, travelers can visit the Church of the Transfiguration at Mount Tabor's summit.

Jordan River

It flows 156 miles south from the Sea of Galilee to the Dead Sea, but the most famous point along its shores is Qasr al-Yahud, where Jesus was baptized by St. John the Baptist. This spot is also said to be where Joshua led the Israelites across the river into the Promised Land of Canaan. Today, many visitors flock to the site, which is 30 miles east of Jerusalem, where they themselves can be baptized. There are several areas available for worship, along with on-site showers and baptismal robes (available for about $8).

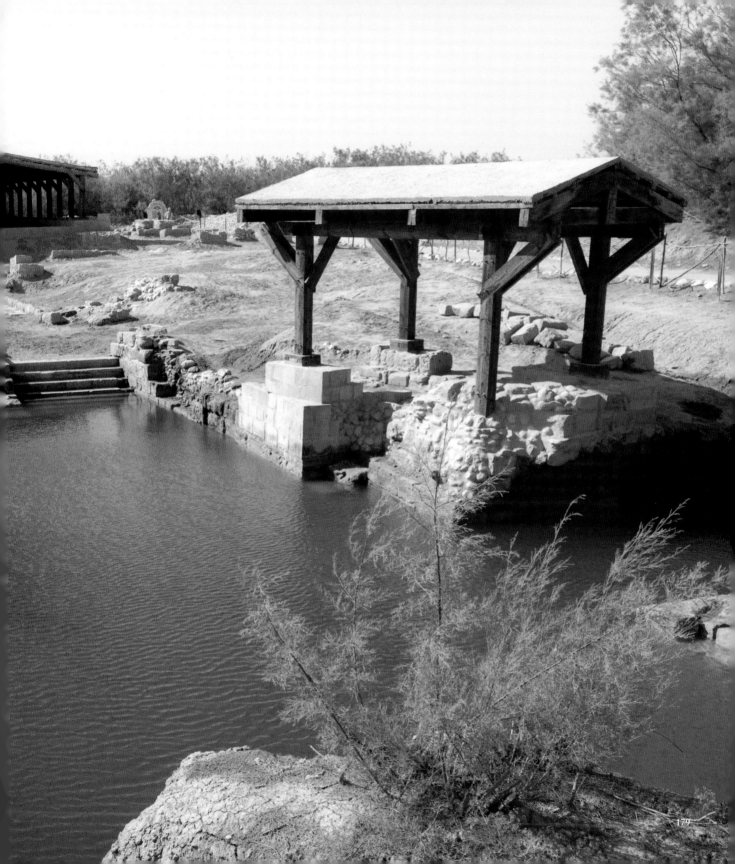

Old Cairo

After fleeing Herod, the Holy Family journeyed to Old
Cairo. They took refuge in a cave under the place where
the Church of Abu Serga now stands; though their stay
here was brief, it remains a popular pilgrimage spot
for Christians from around the world. Tourists can also
visit the ruins of the Fortress of Babylon, dating back
to the 19th century B.C. Within its walls are six Coptic
churches, including the stunning fifth-century Hanging
Church, which features 110 icons and is the site of several
reported apparitions of the Virgin.

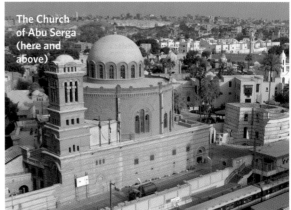

The Church
of Abu Serga
(here and
above)

The Virgin Tree

On their sojourn in Egypt, the Holy Family also stayed in the town of Heliopolis. Legend has it that all the town's idols were destroyed when they arrived, angering the locals, so the Holy Family is said to have sought refuge under a sycamore tree. The original Virgin Tree has been dead for centuries, but two generations of trees have grown out of its former shell.

Monastery of the Holy Virgin

While in Egypt, the Holy Family also lived in a cave in the village of Dayr al-Muharraq, 200 miles south of Cairo, for six months. While they were staying here, an angel appeared to Joseph and said, "Arise, and take the young child and his mother, and go into the land of Israel." In the eighth century, the Monastery of the Holy Virgin was built on what is thought to be that site.

Mount Sinai

It is believed that God presented Moses with the Ten Commandments on this peak, which rises 7,500 feet on the Sinai Peninsula of Egypt. Today, travelers can visit the Monastery of St. Catherine, perhaps the world's oldest continuously inhabited Christian monastery, which was built at its base in the sixth century. Companies like *desertecotours.com* can organize tours from Egypt or Israel.

INDEX

A

Aaron (son of Jochebed), 41
Abel (son of Eve), 16
Abigail, 76-77
Abraham (husband of Sarah), 19–21
Absalom (brother of Tamar), 69
Acts
    9:40–42, 118
    16:14–15, 122
    18:2–3, 124
Adam, 13, 16
Adulterous woman, forgiven by Jesus, 86, 87
Ahab (husband of Jezebel), 71
Amnon (half-brother of Tamar), 68–69
Angels, appearances of, 8, 22, 95, 96, 109, 111, 183. *S*
      See also Gabriel (angel)
Annunciation, 93, 95, 96
Anonymous women, stories in Bible about, 80–87
Aquila (husband of Priscilla), 124, 125
Athaliah (daughter of Jezebel), 73

B

Baal, false gods of, 8, 71
Baptisms, at Qasr al-Yahud, 178
Basilica of the National Shrine of the Immaculate
    Conception, Washington, D.C., 144, 145
Bathsheba, 66–67
Bethlehem, 168–169
Black Madonna
    of Częstochowa, Poland, 148
    Virgin of Regla, Cuba, 152–153
Boaz, 51, 58, 60
Bulrushes, Moses hidden among, 41, 43

C

Cain (son of Eve), 16
Capernaum, Israel, 176
Christian Quarter, Jerusalem, 162
2 Chronicles 22:10–11, 72
Church of Abu Serga, Cairo, 180
Church of St. Anne, Jerusalem, 95
Church of St. Peter in Gallicantu, Jerusalem, 161
Church of the Holy Sepulchre, Jerusalem, 138–139, 164–165
Church of the Sepulchre of Saint Mary, Jerusalem, 101
Clifden, Ireland, shrine in, 156–157
Crucifixion, of Jesus, 98, 106

D

David (king of the Israelites), 51, 66–67
Dayr al-Muharraq, Egypt, 183

Dead Sea, legend of Lot's wife and, 80
Deborah, 52–53
Delilah, 8, 62–63
Diego, Juan, 146, 155
Dormition Abbey, Jerusalem, 160–161
Dyers, patroness of, 122

E

Egypt
    Holy Family in, 180, 183
    Jews escape from, Miriam leads celebration, 10–11, 42–45
Elijah (prophet), 71
Elizabeth (cousin of Mary), 88, 110–111
Endor, witch of, 84
Equality, in early Christian church, 126–127
Esau (son of Isaac), 31
Esther, 78–79
Esther 2:7, 79
Eve, 12–17
Exodus
    1:17–18, 38
    2:2–3, 40
    15:21, 45
    2:21–22, 47

F

Feast days, Marian, 149
Female prophets, 75
    Abigail, 76-77
    Deborah, 52–53
    Esther, 78–79
    Hannah, 64–65
    Huldah, 74–75
    Miriam, 10–11, 42–45
    Sarah, 18–21
Female saints, 128–137
    Bernadette (1844–1879), 132
    Brigid of Ireland (*circa* 453–524), 129, 134–135
    Catherine of Siena (1347–1380), 130
    Elizabeth Ann Seton (1744–1821), 134
    Faustina (1905–1938), 136–137
    Kateri Tekakwitha (1656–1680), 136–137
    Monica (*circa* 322–387), 136–137
    Teresa of Ávila (1515–1582), 130
    Teresa of Calcutta (Mother Teresa), 130–131
    Thérèse of Lisieux (1873–1897), 130

G

Gabriel (angel), 93, 95, 97, 111, 171
Galilee, Sea of, 172–173

Garden of Eden, Adam and Eve in, 13
  banishment from, 14–16
Genesis
  3:6, 12–17
  3:23, 12–17
  21:1–3, 20
  16:3, 23
  24:18–19, 27
  29:16–17, 32
  30:1, 34–37
  27:15 & 17, 29
Genocide, of male Hebrew babies, 39

H
Hagar, 8, 20, 22–23
Hannah (mother of Samuel), 64–65
Hemorrhages, cure of woman suffering from, 85, 86
Herod Antipas (king/ruler of Galilee), 114–116
Herodias (mother of Salome; wife of King Herod Antipas),
  114–116
Hoglah (daughter of Zelophehad), 48–49
Holy days, Marian feast days, 149
Holy Land, important sites in, 160–185
Holy Sepulchre, Church of the, Jerusalem, 138–139,
  164–165
Holy Virgin, monastery of the, Egypt, 182–183
Household gods, Rachel steals, 34, 36
Huldah (female prophet), 74–75
Humanity, "original sin" of, 16

I
Inheritance of land, Zelophehad's daughters petition
  Moses about, 48–49
Isaac (son of Sarah), 8, 20
Ishmael (son of Hagar), 8, 22
Israelite spies, Rahab shelters, 50–51
Israelite women, Miriam leads, 10–11, 43–45

J
Jacob (son of Isaac), 8
  first wife of (Leah), 30–33
  second wife of (Rachel), 34–37
Jael, 54–55
Jehosheba, 72–73
Jericho, battle of, 51
Jerusalem, Israel
  Christian Quarter, 162
  Church of St. Anne, Jerusalem, 95
  Church of St. Peter in Gallicantu, 161
  Church of the Holy Sepulchre, 135–136, 164–165

Church of the Sepulchre of Saint Mary, 101
Dormition Abbey, 160–161
Mount of Olives, 163
Mount Zion, 160–161
Jesus
  baptism at Qasr al-Yahud, 178
  birth of, 95, 97
  crucifixion of, 98, 106
  Mary Magdalene at the tomb of, 104, 106,109
  mourners, 106–107
  resurrection of, 109
  Transfiguration of, 177
  women cured/forgiven by, 86, 87
Jezebel, 8, 70–71
Joan of Arc (1412–1431), 132, 133
Joash (nephew of Jehosheba), 73
Jochebed (mother of Moses), 40–41, 82
John
  19:25, 99
  20:1, 109
  11:21–22, 113
  14:6–7, 114
John the Baptist (son of Elizabeth), 111
  arrest and death of, 114–117
Jordan River, 178–179
Joseph (husband of Mary), 95
Joseph (son of Rachel), 8, 34
Joshua 2:3–4, 50
Joshua (leader of the Israelites), battle of Jericho and, 51
Judges
  4:9, 53
  5:24–26, 54
  5:21, 55
  16:18, 62
Junia [Junias] (female apostle), 120–121

K
Kadesh, Miriam's death in the, 45
Kilbride (place name), meaning of, 135
2 Kings
  9:36–37, 70
  22:14–17, 74

L
Laban (father of Leah and Rachel), 31–32
Lazarus (brother of Martha), 112–113
Leah (sister of Rachel; first wife of Jacob), 8, 30–33
Lily of the Mohawks (St. Kateri Tekakwitha), 136–137
"The Little Flower" (St. Thérèse of Lisieux), 130
Little Way spiritual practice, 130

Lot's wife, legend of, 80, 82
Luke
    1:46–47, 97
    2:7, 97
    8:1–2, 106
    1:36–37, 110
Lydia, 122–123

M

Madonna and Child (drawing by Michelangelo), 94
Madonna of Misericordia, 9
Mahlah (daughter of Zelophehad), 48–49
Male Hebrew babies, execution of, 39, 41
Marian feast days, 149
Marian parades/processions, 152–159
    in Clifden, Ireland, 156–157
    in Cuba, 152–153
    in Mexico City, 154–155
    in Rome, Sri Lankan pilgrims at, 158–159
Marian shrines, 140–141
    Basilica of the National Shrine of the Immaculate
        Conception, Washington, D.C., 144, 145
    Black Madonna of Częstochowa, Poland, 148
    in Clifden, Ireland, 156–157
    Our Lady of Guadalupe shrine, Mexico, 146–147
    Our Lady of La Leche, Florida, 142–143
    Our Lady of Lourdes shrine, France, 140–142
    Our Lady of the Sacred Heart, France, 146
    Sanctuary of our Lady of Fátima, Portugal, 144, 145
Marian statues
    Virgen de la Paz, Venezuela, 144
    Virgen del Socavón, Bolivia, 144
    Virgin of El Rocío, Spain, 150–151
Mark 6:21, 116
Martha (sister of Lazarus), 112–113
Mary (mother of Jesus), 6, 8, 88, 90–101
    birthplace of, 95
    events celebrating/honoring. *See* Marian feast days;
        Marian parades/processions
    mentions in New Testament, 98
    shrines dedicated to. *See* Marian shrines
    statues of. *See* Marian statues
    titles used for, 100
    tomb of, 101
Mary Magdalene, 102–109
Menstruation, in Jewish law, 36, 37
Mexico City, Mexico, Our Lady of Guadalupe shrine in,
    146–147
    procession honoring, 154–155
Milcah (daughter of Zelophehad), 48–49

Miracles. *See also* Resurrection
    of Jesus, 85, 86, 104, 172, 176
    of Mary, 141. *See also* Marian shrines
    Moses extracts water from stone, 45
Miriam (daughter of Jochebed; sister of Moses),
        10–11, 41, 42–45
Misericordia, Madonna of, 9
Modern spirituality, 138–157
Monasteries
    of the Holy Virgin, Egypt, 182–183
    of St. Catherine, Egypt, 184
    St. George's, West Bank, Palestine, 174–175
Mordecai (uncle of Esther), 79
Moses (son of Jochebed)
    daughters of Zelophehad petition, 48–49
    marries Zipporah, 46–47
    rescued by Pharaoh's daughter, 41, 43, 82–83
Mother Teresa (St. Theresa of Calcutta), 130–131
Mount of Olives, Jerusalem, 163
Mount Sinai, Egypt, 184–185
Mount Tabor, Israel, 177
Mount Zion, Jerusalem, 160–161

N

Nameless women, stories in Bible about, 80–87
Naomi (mother-in-law to Ruth and Orpah), 56–61
Nathan (prophet), 67
Nazareth, Israel, 170–171
New Testament, women of, 88–127
Newborn Hebrew boys, execution ordered, 39, 41
Nile River, 41, 43
Noa (daughter of Zelophehad), 48–49
Numbers 27:7, 48

O

Obed (son of Ruth), 58, 60
Old Testament, women of, 10–87
"Original sin," 16
Orpah (Naomi's daughter-in-law), 58
Our Lady of Guadalupe shrine, Mexico, 146–147
Our Lady of La Leche shrine, Florida, 142–143
Our Lady of Lourdes shrine, France, 140–142
    St. Bernadette and, 132
Our Lady of the Sacred Heart shrine, France, 146

P

Parades. *See* Marian parades/processions
Paul (apostle), women associated with, 120–127
Peter (apostle), 109, 176
    resurrection of Tabitha, 118, 119

Pharaoh
    daughter of, as Moses's rescuer, 41, 43, 82–83
    reign of terror over Jews, 39, 41
Phoebe, as Paul's emissary to Rome, 126–127
Pietà (sculpture by Michelangelo), 99
Pontius Pilate's wife, 86
Potiphar's wife, 82
Priscilla [Prisca], 124–125
Processions. *See* Marian parades/processions
Puah (midwife), 38–39, 41
Purim, founding of, 79

Q
Qasr al-Yahud, baptisms at, 178
Queen of Sheba, 84

R
Rachel (sister of Leah; second wife of Jacob), 8, 31–32, 34–35
    as Jacob's second wife, 34–37
Rahab, 50–51
Rebecca [Rebekah], 8, 24–29
Red Sea, parting of, 43
Repentant woman, forgiven by Jesus, 86
Resurrection
    of Jesus, 109
    of Lazarus, 112–113
    of Tabitha, 118–119
Romans
    16:7, 120–121
    16:1–2, 126
Ruth
    1:15–16, 58
    3:8–9, 60
Ruth (Naomi's daughter-in-law), 56–61

S
St. Catherine, monastery of, Egypt, 182–183
St. George's Monastery, West Bank, Palestine, 174–175
Saints, female. *See* Female saints
Salome (daughter of Herodias), 8, 114–117
Samaritan woman at the well, conversion of, 85, 86
Samson, 62–63
Samuel 2:21, 65
1 Samuel 25:32-33, 76
2 Samuel
    11:2-3, 67
    13:12–13, 68
Samuel (son of Hannah), 64–65
Sanctuary of our Lady of Fátima, Portugal, 144, 145

Sarah (wife of Abraham), 8, 18–21
Sea of Galilee, 172–173
Seth (son of Eve), 16
Sexual equality, in early Christian church, 126–127
Sheba, queen of, 84
Shiphrah (midwife), 38–39, 41
Shrines, to the Virgin Mary. *See* Marian shrines
Siserra, assassination of, 54–55
Solomon (son of Bathsheba), 66
Spiritual life/Spirituality
    elements of, 112
    the Little Way, 130
    modern, 138–157
Stations of the Cross, 166–167
Statues, of the Virgin Mary. *See* Marian statues

T
Tabitha [Dorcas], resurrection of, 118–119
Tamar (daughter of King David), 68–69
Tirzah (daughter of Zelophehad), 48–49
Tomb, of Mary, 101
Transfiguration, of Jesus, 177
Tribes of Israel
    census of, 49
    founding of, 32

U
Uriah (husband of Bathsheba), 67

V
Via Dolorosa (Stations of the Cross), 166–167
Virgen de la Paz statue, Venezuela, 144
Virgen del Socavón statue, Bolivia, 144, 145
Virgin of El Rocío statue, Spain, 150–151
Virgin of Regla (Black Madonna), Cuba, 152–153
The Virgin Tree, 181

W
Water, as motif in Miriam's life, 45
Way of Suffering (Stations of the Cross), 166–167
Wells, significant events/meetings at, 22, 24, 30, 34, 46, 85, 86
Witch of Endor, 84

Z
Zechariah (husband of Elizabeth), 111
Zelophehad, daughters of, 48–49
Zipporah (wife of Moses), 46–47

CREDITS

COVER Pascal Deloche/Getty Images **INSIDE FLAP** Heritage Images/Getty Images **1** Wikimedia **2-3** JLGutierrez/ Getty Images **5** Print Collector/Getty Images **6-7** Leemage/Getty Images **9** Heritage Images/Getty Images **10-11** DEA/L. PEDICINI/Getty Images **12** Alinari Archives/Getty Images **14-15** Lebrecht Music & Arts/Alamy **17** PHAS/Getty Images **18** DEA/L. PEDICINI/Getty Images **20-21** Alfredo Dagli Orti/Shutterstock **23** DEA/ L. PEDICINI/Getty Images **24** The Art Archive/Shutterstock **26-27** Gianni Dagli Orti/Shutterstock **28-29** Leemage/ Getty Images; UniversalImagesGroup/Getty Images **30** DEA/L. PEDICINI/Getty Images **32-33** Universal History Archive/Getty Images **35** DEA/L. PEDICINI/Getty Images **36-37** Universal History Archive/Getty Images; Heritage Images/Getty Images **38** Superstock/Everett **40** jozef sedmak/Alamy **42** Heritage Images/Getty Images **44-45** Album/Alamy **46-47** Vincenzo Fontana/Getty Images **48-49** Lebrecht Music and Arts Photo Library/Alamy **50** Art Directors & TRIP/Alamy **53** UniversalImagesGroup/Getty Images **54** Heritage Image Partnership Ltd/Alamy **56-57** Print Collector/Getty Images **59-61** Lebrecht Music and Arts Photo Library/Alamy (2) **62** Gianni Dagli Orti/ Shutterstock **65** Lebrecht Music and Arts Photo Library/Alamy **67** Peter Horree/Alamy **68** Heritage Images/Getty Images **70** PHAS/Getty Images **72** SeM/Getty Images **74** ZU_09/Getty Images **76** IanDagnall Computing/Alamy **78** Heritage Images/Getty Images **80-81** Reza/Getty Images **82-83** Historical Picture Archive/Getty Images **84** Buyenlarge/Getty Images **85** Universal History Archive/Getty Images **86** Historia/Shutterstock **87** Alinari Archives/Getty Images **88-89** Mondadori Portfolio/Getty Images **90-91** Heritage Images/Getty Images **92** Print Collector/Getty Images **93** Geography Photos/Getty Images **94** Heritage Images/Getty Images **95** PRISMA ARCHIVO/Alamy **96** Heritage Images/Getty Images **97** DEA/G. NIMATALLAH/Getty Images **98** Heritage Images/Getty Images **99** Leemage/Getty Images **100** imageBROKER/Shutterstock **101** DEA/S. VANNINI/Getty Images **102-103** Print Collector/Getty Images **104** Alinari Archives/Getty Images **105** Mondadori Portfolio/Getty Images **106-107** Thekla Clark/Getty Images **108** Alamy **110-115** Heritage Images/Getty Images (3) **116** Gianni Dagli Orti/Shutterstock **117** Heritage Images/Getty Images **118** jozef sedmak/Alamy **120** History and Art Collection/Alamy **122** Buyenlarge/Getty Images **124** Zvonimir Atletic/Alamy **126** Art Directors & TRIP/Alamy **128-129** Mary Evans/ Shutterstock **130-131** Alfredo Dagli Orti/Shutterstock; Tim Graham/Getty Images **132** United Archives/Getty Images **133** DEA/G. DAGLI ORTI/Getty Images **134** Hulton Archive/Getty Images **135** David Lyons/Alamy **136** Mondadori Portfolio/Getty Images; DEA/G. DAGLI ORTI/Getty Images **137** Robert Alexander/Getty Images **138-139** Jon Arnold Images/Alamy **140-141** Andia/Getty Images **142-143** EQRoy/Alamy **144-145** Clockwise from left: Gerard SIOEN/Getty Images; Alexis DUCLOS/Getty Images; Alex Arnold/Alamy; AIZAR RALDES/Getty Images **146** Eric D ricochet69/Alamy **147** Lucas Vallecillos/AP Photo **148** Best View Stock/Alamy **149** Bill Clark/Getty Images **150-151** Juan Aunion/Alamy **152-153** YAMIL LAGE/Getty Images **154-155** Pacific Press/Getty Images **156-157** Tim Graham/Getty Images **158-159** Stefano Montesi/Corbis/Getty Images **160-161** RnDmS/Alamy **162-163** Clockwise from bottom left: Craig Stennett/Alamy; Image Professionals GmbH/Alamy; Rostislav Glinsky/Alamy **164-165** Abir Sultan/EPA/Shutterstock **166-167** Dominika Zarzycka/Alamy; Via del Rosa/Alamy **168-169** Jason Langley/Alamy **170-171** eFesenko/Alamy; DEA/ARCHIVIO J. LANGE/Getty Images **172-173** RnDmS/Alamy **174-175** PhotoStock-Israel/Alamy **176** Ruslan Kalnitsky/Alamy **177** Brian Maudsley/Alamy **178-179** Alatom/Getty Images **180-181** Clockwise from bottom left: Patrick CHAPUIS/Getty Images; Peter Horree/Alamy; Mike Nelson/EPA/Shutterstock **182-183** Xinhua/Alamy **184-185** Martin van Doorn/Alamy **BACK COVER** Clockwise from left: Heritage Images/Getty Images; Ian Dagnall/Alamy; Alamy, Heritage/Getty Images

Special thanks to contributing writers Anne Marie O'Connor and Joanna Powell

CENTENNIAL BOOKS

An Imprint of
Centennial Media, LLC
40 Worth St., 10th Floor
New York, NY 10013, U.S.A.

CENTENNIAL BOOKS is a trademark of Centennial Media, LLC

ISBN 978-1-951274-44-3

Distributed by
Simon & Schuster, Inc.
1230 Avenue of the Americas
New York, NY 10020, U.S.A.

For information about custom editions, special sales and premium and corporate purchases,
please contact Centennial Media at contact@centennialmedia.com.

Manufactured in Malaysia

© 2020 by Centennial Media, LLC

10 9 8 7 6 5 4 3 2 1

Publishers & Co-Founders Ben Harris, Sebastian Raatz
Editorial Director Annabel Vered
Creative Director Jessica Power
Executive Editor Janet Giovanelli
Deputy Editors Ron Kelly, Alyssa Shaffer
Design Director Ben Margherita
Art Directors Andrea Lukeman,
Natali Suasnavas, Joseph Ulatowski
Assistant Art Director Jaclyn Loney
Photo Editor Christina Creutz
Production Manager Paul Rodina
Production Assistant Alyssa Swiderski
Editorial Assistant Tiana Schippa
Sales & Marketing Jeremy Nurnberg